ML 652 .B6 194

W9-DEJ-187

Blom, Eric, 1888-1959.

The romance of the piano

MN

Library of Congress

Fairleigh Dickinson University Library
Teaneck, New Jersey

THE ROMANCE
OF THE PIANO

Da Capo Press Music Reprint Series

GENERAL EDITOR

FREDERICK FREEDMAN

VASSAR COLLEGE

THE ROMANCE OF THE PIANO

By Eric Blom

Fairleigh Dickinson
University Library

Teaneck, New Jersey

193129

DA CAPO PRESS • NEW YORK • 1969

ML
652
.B6
1969

Fairleigh Dickinson
University Library

Teaneck, New Jersey

A Da Capo Press Reprint Edition

This Da Capo Press edition of *The Romance of the Piano*
is an unabridged republication
of the first edition published
in London in 1928. It is reprinted by
special arrangement with G. T. Foulis & Co. Ltd.

Library of Congress Catalog Card Number   69-15608

A Division of Plenum Publishing Corporation
227 West 17th Street
New York, N.Y. 10011
All rights reserved

Printed in the United States of America

MC
692
B6

1926

THE ROMANCE
OF THE PIANO

VERMEER: LADY SEATED AT THE HARPSICHORD

National Gallery

THE ROMANCE
OF THE PIANO

BY

ERIC BLOM

AUTHOR OF
"STEPCHILDREN OF MUSIC," "THE LIMITATIONS OF MUSIC."

PUBLISHERS : FOULIS : LONDON
SEVEN MILFORD LANE, W.C.2.

Printed in Great Britain by
The Marshall Press Ltd., London, W.C.2.

TO
MICHAEL AND CELIA

CONTENTS

ILLUSTRATIONS

INTRODUCTION

WHEN the Publishers asked me more than four years ago—this book has been held up for various reasons —to write the story of the piano, I had good cause to hesitate before I accepted the commission. For one thing, it seemed to me that the subject had been exhausted by previous writers; for another, I did not feel that, seeing how carefully it had been dealt with by specialists, a critic whose business it is to know everything and whose misfortune never to know enough, could do justice to what is after all but one current in the vast stream of musical history. Yielding so far to persuasion, however, as to survey the field to be explored with some thoroughness, I came to the conclusion that perhaps it would still be possible to write about the evolution of the modern household instrument in a way sufficiently new to justify a fresh investigation of the whole ground of research, and this without impertinent pretence to supersede the specialists. Eventually the task began to look fascinating, and I decided to undertake it.

It is hoped that the little book which is the outcome of a good deal of laborious study will not read like a mere agglomeration of the facts

INTRODUCTION

that had perforce to be somehow adduced in the course of the story. They cannot even claim to be new facts, since truth, once told, can only be repeated and may not be manufactured afresh for the sake of picturesqueness. So far romance dare not go in a case like this. But I have endeavoured to produce an effect of novelty by treating the available material as it does not appear to have been treated before. The development of the piano and the characteristics of the instruments which led to it seem to me to have been too often described in so elaborately technical a language that the information could not help becoming a little dry. Those generally interested in music, and the young people for whom this book is mainly intended, could perhaps hardly be expected to be thrilled by such an array of scientific evidence. The plain history of the piano, it might be said, has been often written, and better than I could have done it; what I attempted to do was to show that this history is charged with romance, and romance that can be none the less exciting because it is made to tell, as I hope it is here, the truth at every turn. The procedure was really quite simple : it was only a matter of relating the instrument's story constantly

INTRODUCTION

to the art and culture of which it is the messenger instead of giving a detached narrative of the progress it made as a mechanical contrivance and a piece of furniture. That must be the all-round critic's excuse for tackling this special subject. If this little book deepens the reader's love of music while awakening his interest in what is only one of music's carriers, it will have done all it set out to do.

My thanks are due to many people for kind and valuable collaboration in the choice of illustrations, notably to my wife for research work done, to Mr. Herbert Lambert for permission to reproduce one of his beautiful camera portraits, to the Editor of *The Music Teacher* for several suggestions, to Messrs. Broadwood for the portrait of Burkat Shudi and to Messrs. Steinway for one of their admirable drawings.

London,   E.B.
September, 1928.

I. REMOTE ANCESTRY

I. REMOTE ANCESTRY

THE unimaginative seldom pause before a modern piano to reflect that it has a romantic history. They accept its perfections without bestowing much thought on its gradual evolution through a line of ancestors reaching back to a time so remote that it is only lost to human perception where history itself grows dim. The highly intricate organism of the most widely used musical instrument of to-day is too often taken for granted with scarcely any desire to know how it came into being—indeed with hardly the sign of any wish to examine and understand its mechanism. Perhaps this lack of curiosity is a proof of healthy affection. We shrink from dissecting the things we love. Who thinks, on listening to *Tristan and Isolde*, of seeking under the complex psychology of Wagner's poem the ancient and elemental Celtic legend from which it is derived, or of watching his music for traces of the countless and mysteriously linked-up influences, the causes and effects of musical progress, without which it would not have been what it is ?

Our modern everyday life rarely allows us to look beneath the surface of things. The piano is to most of us a piece of furniture, a necessary adjunct to the household, of doubtful ornamental value, but to be tolerated as a not too irksome levy to pay for the privilege of being civilised. True, to some of us it is also a solace and a companionable source of interest, but just because the pleasure and instruction it yields are so infinite, we have neither time nor inclination to inquire into the constitution and the ancestry of the giver. Every object or utensil in the household, after all, is richly laden with a history of the manners and cultures of the past, and it may be argued that, if there is indeed any profit to be derived from an inquiry into the antecedents of things, we might as well study the romance of the inkpot as that of the piano. And why not ? The evolution of the inkpot may have perceptibly influenced that of literature. Its fore-bear, the inkhorn, could be slung over the shoulder and taken into the open air, and would therefore conceivably lead the writer to produce by direct observation and experience of life ; the static inkpot, on the other hand, would induce a seden-tary mode of production, a studious, contemplative and deductive way of writing. If so simple an object can be imagined to have swayed the art with which it is connected in the loosest and most casual way, how much more must the course of

4

REMOTE ANCESTRY

music have been affected by the implement without which a whole important category of it could never have existed. To know nothing of the development of musical instruments is to ignore the historical growth of music itself.

In tracing the piano back to its earliest sources, we grope about in periods on which history keeps eternal silence. The piano is the offspring of an alliance between the two separate families of percussion and of string instruments, both established before the earliest times of which we have any human records. Their primordial forms can only be conjectured. The percussion instruments, it is true, have retained much of their primitive nature ; a skin stretched by a savage over a hollowed gourd essentially differs from our modern kettle-drum only in the latter's mechanism for obtaining notes of definite pitch. But the far-off ancestry of string instruments is more difficult to determine in proportion to the vastly greater strides they have made towards subtlety of musical expression and perfection of technique. The probability is that an early huntsman with an ear for music discovered that the string of his bow, directly the arrow was released, gave out a whirring and uncertain note. The bow, perhaps, had been

ROMANCE OF THE PIANO

made from a wood that was too inelastic for the purpose of the chase, but gave out something like a musical sound precisely because of its rigidity. The inference naturally drawn by an inventive mind would be that the more unyielding the wood, the clearer the ring of the note produced.* Experiments with various harder materials would, incidentally, lead to the conclusion that slight divergencies in the length of the string produced notes of different pitch, and that a collection of such one-stringed bows of graded sizes could be placed together and made to yield some kind of musical scale.

From this point it was but one step farther, but a step it may have taken centuries to take, to the revelation that several strings could be stretched upon one and the same bow, since its curve naturally graduated their length and so differentiated their pitch. As the tension on the bow was thus increased, it had to be proportionately strengthened by greater thickness, but strangely enough the most obvious means of

---

* With such facility Ulysses bent
His own huge bow, and with his right hand play'd
The nerve, which in its quick vibration sang
Clear as the swallow's voice.

Odyssey (Cowper's translation), Book XXI.

support, the front pillar, was n
much later.* On the earliest p
tions of the harp it is invariably

The three nations with the
known to history, Assyria, Eg
possessed harps of various typ
have left us sculptures and paintings which permit
no uncertainty as to the shape of their instruments,
but there is considerable doubt with regard to the
nature of the Hebrew instruments. The exact
application of the names in the Bible is uncertain
even in the original, and more so in the translations, which often use the nomenclature of instruments current in their own periods. Carl Engel†
pointed out that some of the instruments mentioned in the Book of Daniel in Chaldean, the
language adopted by the Jews during the
Babylonian captivity, may be synonymous with
some of the Hebrew names appearing elsewhere
in the Old Testament. The music of the Israelites
owed much to that of Assyria and Egypt, although
the influence produced merely an extension of

* The Irish harp, of which the front pillar is so prominent
a feature, has recently been proved to have existed without it
at first. Its discovery seems to be of Celtic origin, but it may have
been imported from the East. As in many similar cases,
independent discovery in various quarters of the globe is probable.
† Carl Engel, *The Music of the Most Ancient Nations*, 1864.

ir own means and not a new acquisition. With the music of these neighbouring countries their instruments, including the harp, would naturally be imported into Palestine, unless, as is more probable, similar ones already existed there.

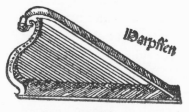

HARP

The Assyrian harp was held or hung against the musician's breast and thus enabled him to move about freely while playing it. The Egyptian harps, on the other hand, which were made in a great variety of sizes and shapes, stood on the floor if they were large or on a stand if smaller, and were played in an upright or crouching position. Since at later stages of musical history we can trace a distinct connexion between the nature of instruments and that of the music played on them, it seems by no means too fantastic to infer a similar dependence at this obscure period, and to hazard a guess that Assyrian music must have

8

been predominantly martial and ceremonious and that of Egypt pacific and intimate.

Closely allied with the harp is the lyre, and as an intermediary between these two types stands the trigonon, a triangular instrument spread throughout ancient Egypt and overlapping into Greece. According to Sophocles, the lyre was especially a Phrygian inhabitant, but to the modern world it is the musical instrument most intimately associated with the whole of classical Greek culture. The Greeks attributed its invention to Mercury, who was said to have constructed it from the shell of a tortoise found on the banks of the Nile. The fact is that it existed both in Egypt and in Asia long before the Greeks knew it. There are lyres to be seen on Assyrian sculptures dating from about 1000 B.C.

The Greek lyre had at different times four, seven and ten strings, which were plucked with a plectrum, the forebear, not only of a similar implement still used with the mandoline and the zither, but also of the harpsichord quill. The player's left hand, however, touched the strings with the finger tips, harp-fashion. The smaller lyres were held by the left arm or between the knees, and the larger, deeper-toned instruments supported by a ribbon slung across the shoulder or by a loop thrown over the left hand.

Such are the early ancestors from whom the piano inherited its array of strings placed next to each other so as to yield a musical scale. But the piano is not purely a string instrument ; it is also a percussion instrument, and we have now to examine another branch of the family from whose mixed marriage it has sprung. We have already seen how a primitive kettle-drum was constructed from a gourd and the skin of some animal or another. The next discovery, made probably in Asia, and most likely in Persia or Arabia, was that definite notes could be obtained from an instrument made on the drum pattern from a hollow piece of wood or a calabash, by stretching strings of vegetable fibre or animal hair across the opening. Although the thought of plucking these strings with the finger tips must have obtruded itself before long, it is nevertheless easily imagined that the percussive mode of performing was retained in preference, for the East hugs its conventions with a peculiar obstinacy. Even now a stringed percussion instrument of this type, called the santir, survives in the Orient, especially in the Caucasus.

REMOTE ANCESTRY

The next thing was to find means of temporarily altering the length of the strings and consequently their pitch at the player's discretion, and this was contrived by the addition of a neck or fingerboard to the instrument, which diverted it into the lute family and, at a still later stage, by the addition of the bow, into the viol group. But although the santir thus perpetuated itself in a branch altogether remote from the lineage to which this study is devoted, it still has one or two direct, if inglorious, descendants in Europe. They are instrument of the dulcimer type. The mediæval Italians had an instrument of the kind which they called *stromento di porco* (pig instrument), and its German relative was known as *Schweinskopf*. The shape at that time was certainly not unlike that of a pig's head seen in profile, and the resemblance was rendered more striking by a round sound-hole placed in a position on the soundboard corresponding to that of the animal's eye. By the eighteenth century, however, the instrument had assumed a trapeze shape, which still allowed strings of varying lengths to be drawn across it, and the Germans now called it, even more appropriately, *Hackbrett* (chopping board). The Italian term of that period, *salterio tedesco* (German psaltery), although inaccurate, at any rate has its use in pointing to the region where the instrument had the greatest vogue. During the last years of the seventeenth century, Pantaleon Hebenstreit, a native of Eisleben, became a virtuoso on the dulcimer, and having attained to extraordinary proficiency on it, he built an exceptionally elaborate model for himself. He went to Paris in 1705 and so enchanted Louis XIV by his playing that he won high distinction at the court, and the dulcimer, at the instigation of the king, came to be called *pantaléon* in France.

DULCIMER

The dulcimer had brass or iron wires which were struck with hammers, and gradations of tone could be produced not only by regulating the force of the blow, but by harder and softer coverings on the extremities of the hammers.

REMOTE ANCESTRY

Matteson said in 1717 that the dulcimer had greater dynamic variety than either the harpsichord or the clavichord. Its great defect was the absence of any damping contrivance to check the vibration of the strings at will. The effect must have been as unpleasant as that of the piano played with the pedal permanently pressed down. Schubert imitated the instrument in his *Divertissement à la Hongroise* for piano duet, and pianists who wish to reproduce it realistically may be allowed for once to fall temporarily into this most exasperating of habits cultivated by brazen incompetence.

The dulcimer, a prototype of which is to be seen on the early Assyrian sculptures in the British Museum—once again we have to look back to that musical and military nation—now only survives as a national instrument among the Hungarian and Transylvanian gipsies under the Magyar name of *cimbalom*. The rest of Europe only looks upon it cursorily with the mixture of curiosity and pity occasionally vouchsafed to a freak. It is to music what Punch and Judy are to the drama : fit to amuse an idle theatre queue, but left behind and forgotten as soon as there is something better at hand. Nevertheless, one or

13

two recent attempts have been made to revive it. A descendant of Hebenstreit's gives astonishing performances on the instrument he calls a *tympanon*, Stravinsky wrote a part for it in his "Ragtime" for small orchestra, and Kodály in his Opera, "Hary Janos."

Akin to the dulcimer is the psaltery, an instrument now extinct, but once widely diffused in various forms. The feature that chiefly distinguished it from its relative was the plectrum with which the strings were plucked. Like the lyre, it led thus to the harpsichord quills which twang the strings, whereas the dulcimer, with its hammers, is directly allied to the percussion instrument which Beethoven, to indicate its peculiarity and to avoid the Italian musical terminology he abjured towards the end of his career, called the *Hammerclavier*.

The earliest traces of the psaltery are to be found in the old Babylonian sabekka or sambuka, and it is also related to the Persian and Arabic santir and kanun. After its development into the harpsichord, its direct lineage died out from sheer exhaustion, and it has only some comparatively obscure progeny which still makes a rather piteous show in the guise of national

THE PROPHET DAVID WITH PSALTERY.

SAINT CECILIA WITH REGAL.

instruments. In Bavaria and the Tyrol we find it as the zither and in Russia as the goussly.

Yet another instrument, probably the earliest that exploited the principle of strings vibrating

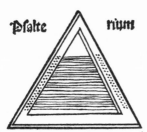

PSALTERY (FROM VIRDUNG, 1511)

over a closed wooden box as distinct from a hollow shape open at one end, must be mentioned as belonging to the promiscuous family from which the piano has come down to us. This is the monochord, a curious half scientific and half musical contrivance, consisting of an elongated

15

wooden case over which, as the instrument's name implies, a single string was drawn lengthwise. The first full description of the monochord occurs in a treatise by Euclid, written about the year 300 B.C., but it was already known to Pythagoras in the second half of the sixth century B.C. In 532 B.C. Pythagoras left the court of the tyrant Polycrates on the island of Samos to visit Egypt and to travel in Asia, where he studied the lore of the Chaldeans and the Magi and may even have reached India. He doubtless acquired his musical knowledge in the East, and the scientific division of the musical scale, based on acoustic principles, was probably imported to Europe by him. It is certain that it was he who settled the distribution of tones and semitones within the octave in the different arrays representing the Greek modes, and if he transported this system from Egypt or the Orient, nothing seems more plausible than that he should have found the monochord there also, for it was this instrument by which the degrees of the scale were scientifically fixed and practically demonstrated. The string, sounding a certain definite note when left to ring freely, would yield the octave above if stopped exactly in the centre in such a way that only half the length vibrated.

REMOTE ANCESTRY

Other intervals were, of course, gained by sub-
dividing the string at mathematical ratios. It is
likely that at first the string was stopped merely
by the finger, as on the modern violin, or possibly
by an implement resembling a screwdriver ;
but later on frets were introduced which automatically fixed the points where the string was to
be intersected, as on the guitar, the banjo and
similar instruments.

Pythagoras seems to have introduced the
musical scale and the monochord not only to
Greece, but also to Italy, where he eventually
settled in the Greek colony of Croton,* founded as
early as 710 B.C. In its adopted country it
seems to have lingered on until, at the end of the
sixth century A.D., when the Church of Rome
began to make a careful study of sacred music, it
was revived to record and preserve the ecclesiastical
modes. It was still in use early in the eleventh
century, when the monk, musician and scientist
Guido d'Arezzo invented a movable bridge
whereby the notes could be automatically fixed.
That the instrument was known far away from
Italy about a century later is proved by its mention
in Wace's *Roman de Brut.*

* The modern Cotrone in Calabria.

ROMANCE OF THE PIANO

Like the dulcimer and the psaltery, the monochord has an obscure survivor to-day, an ignoble degenerate only met with occasionally in the gutter. It is known as the *tromba marina* or marine trumpet, a one-stringed instrument that emits a nasal, shrieking and querulous sound through a kind of gramophone horn. But the monochord has nobler descendants than this mongrel instrument. Both the violin and the lute families are its relatives, and among keyboard instruments the clavichord, where the pitch of each note is adjusted by a temporary stopping of the string, is closely connected with it. But the clavichord is to be discussed in a later chapter.

II. THE COMING OF
THE KEYBOARD

II. THE COMING OF
THE KEYBOARD

THE transition between the primitive instruments outlined in the preceding chapter and the first keyed string instruments is almost as obscure as the missing link between ape and man which biologists still have to establish before they can prove the latter's descent from the former beyond controversy. It cannot even be definitely said whether the keyboard, as we now know it, was taken over by the stringed instruments from the organ or whether it was expressly designed for the early forebears of the piano and subsequently adapted to the keyed wind instrument. That the organ had a keyboard of a kind at a very remote period is certain, but which type of instrument first possessed keys actually resembling in shape and mechanism those of to-day it is impossible to discover. It is scarcely credible that the organ can have had any contrivance capable of being at once transferred to a stringed instrument without considerable modifications, but there is no doubt that certain improvements already existed before the adaptation took place. In all probability there was a fair exchange of valuable suggestion and successful discovery between the two instrumental types.

Such particulars as have come down to us of the hydraulic organ invented by Ctesibius of Alexandria in the second century B.C., an instrument whose pipes were supplied with wind by the pressure of water, give no clue to the method whereby the sound was released—unlocked, it might be said, were it certain that the Latin name for the mechanism that set the sound free could be properly applied to so early an instrument. That Latin name was *clavis*, and English is the only language which still retains its equivalent of " key." In the languages of the other European musical nations the Latin term perpetuated itself in the names they gave to the keyed instruments themselves (*clavicembalo*, *clavecin*, *Clavier*, etc.), but it lost its original application to the keys alone, which became identified with the idea of " touch " (*tasti*, *touches*, *Tasten*).

We know that the organs of the earliest centuries of the Christian era were no longer hydraulic, but already produced their sound by means of bellows. For a long time each pipe seems to have had its own bellow and with organs of considerable size the playing must have been an exceedingly laborious and wasteful procedure. The Saxon church at Winchester, which yielded its place to the Cathedral in 1093, had an organ which is known to have existed by about 980 and is said to have required seventy blowers to keep it supplied with wind.

The keyboards of the Winchester organ and its contemporaries were exceedingly primitive. Until the eleventh century the keys were not pressed down, but drawn in and out. They resembled the sliding lid of a domino box and had a hole which, coming into contact with the aperture of the organ pipe, allowed the wind to pass through the latter. Directly the slide was moved to its original position again, the wind was cut off and the pipe silenced. By the end of the eleventh century the slides were still in use, but they were now governed by a system, scarcely less clumsy than the older device, of levers which had to be pressed down. They were thus the direct forerunners of the more modern keys, with the difference that, once depressed, they remained in that position and left the organ pipe speaking until the player released them by a second effort. There was no question of leaving the finger on the key as long as the note was required, for these

23

ROMANCE OF THE PIANO

early precursors of the keyboard were not made to the scale of the human hand, but to that of the instrument. Each lever was placed directly under the pipe it controlled, and in large organs the keyboard had to be of such dimensions that it might almost have been played in the pedestrian manner in which Gulliver performed on the Brobdingnagian harpsichords. There were organs which had keys from three to five inches in width, up to a yard in length, and with a fall of as much as a foot. It is easily imagined how coarse and unwieldy the music performed on these instruments must have sounded. Its uncouth gait can only have been slightly mitigated by extreme agility on the part of the organist, who had to make desperate lunges, not only to unchain each note in time, but also to cut it off again. He had surely to be as much an athlete as a musician and his performance must have been as strenuous as the practice of a boxer at the punchball, for the keys only yielded to a vigorous blow and could only be replaced by an equally vigorous tug. In Germany, long after the introduction of the modern keyboard, it was the custom to speak of the organ, not as being played but " struck " or " smitten." An organist was an *Orgelschläger*.

COMING OF THE KEYBOARD

As the number of organ pipes augmented, the levers, which still had to be directly attached to them, became more and more unmanageable by their increasing distance from each other. At last, in the twelfth century, means were found of sounding more than one pipe by the action of a single lever. But the subterfuge was a purely mechanical one and as music became more complex, its inadequacy had to be admitted. A succession of several of these hyphenated notes must have yielded hideous progressions. But the age was used to them. Already in the tenth century, Hucbald of St. Amand had fixed down the rules of diaphony, a crude system of rudimentary counterpoint also known under the name of organum, which simply accompanied a melody rigidly a fourth below, an exception being only made, no less inflexibly, at two points of the scale where the interval of the fourth was forbidden as having a bad effect. For the rest, we have Hucbald's assurance that this callow attempt at harmony was wholly pleasing, if sung slowly and with gravity.*

As the organs grew larger and their music more

* New forms of diaphony are used with excellent effect by modern composers, notably Debussy, whose *Cathédrale engloutie* for piano provides a good example.

elaborate, it became imperatively necessary to find means for the organist to gain contact with the pipes by a mechanical device which would leave him leisure enough to devote his attention to what he was playing. His claim to be an interpreter, and not merely a manipulator, had to be met and human ingenuity directed to the task of establishing a system whereby the player could control the pipes without having to run after them.

The little portable organ, known as the regal, had slides, or levers, or whatever the elementary equivalent of the key happened to be at the time, which were adapted to its size and thus naturally under the control of the player's hand. It must have occurred to some logician at one time or another that the rational procedure would be to keep the proportions of the keyboard always adjusted to those of the human hand which directly governed it, instead of varying them according to the size of the instrument.

But it was above all the increasing intricacy of the music that induced the invention of a more tractable keyboard. Thus, with a sublime tyranny, art imposes its will on science and craft. Technical advances are continually produced indirectly by some genius who sets up a goal too high for the mechanical achievements of his time to reach. Fine talents which fall short of productive initiative, but gladly serve under creative leadership, are encouraged by genius to realise his ideals for him on the purely manipulative side. The great artist can only visualise and must leave the materialisation of his visions to others ; but so strong is his prophetic insight that it irresistibly stimulates reproductive inventiveness in others. A Beethoven, on being told that one of his passages cannot be played on the oboe, does not therefore say that he will re-write it until it becomes possible. He has a right to insist, in the face of all practical experience, that by some means or other it has got to be played as he wants it. His productive instinct, aware that art has a reality of a higher and different order from that of daily life, tells him that if he only imagines its practicability clearly enough, someone will be found to make it feasible. A Wagner may suggest scenic miracles like the " Tarnhelm " scene in *Rhinegold* without having the remotest technical notion how they are going to be performed. It is enough for him to want them realised for a few people to set their teeth in determination not to yield until the task is accomplished. Smaller men would simply have to capitulate in such cases, since, failing to do creative work of the highest sort, they would necessarily fail also to incite reproductive work on the same level in those who are waiting to be led.

It should become clear in the course of this study that invention of mechanical improvements always treads on the heels of some fine achievement in musical creation which transcends the capabilities of the available instruments. It is difficult to think of any new device in the art of instrument making which was not suggested by a creative effort, not necessarily in the direction of composition, but often in that of improvisation. The latter, it is easily conjectured, must have been a fertile soil for instrumental improvements to grow upon. The extempore player, anxious to cover up bald patches of flagging invention and to embellish mechanical bridge-passages leading from one haphazard idea to another, would naturally seek to detract attention by superficially pleasing intrumental effects. It would be surprising if the multiplication of organ stops and the invention of similar though more limited contrivances for the harpsichord were not in a

28

large measure due to the instrument makers' desire to extend the improvising musician's range of sham inspiration.

Nevertheless, it must not be imagined that instrumental evolution was a continuous stream of suggestion on the part of musicians and compliance on that of the makers. In the history of music, as in that of mankind, it is not always the sovereign who rules. There are periods during which he will be swayed by his subjects to the extent of accommodating his policy to their collective will. Music as a productive art and its dependants, the instruments, were often in an exactly analogous position. The art at times ruled with a benevolent despotism which spurred its servants on to unceasing effort, but at others it merely adjusted itself to their capabilities and thus induced no improvement in them. Mozart, who had a most sensitive feeling for the treatment of every instrument as it was constituted in his time, wrote always strictly within its capacities, and consequently did nothing to dissatisfy the players with their medium and nothing to annoy the makers into greater enterprise. Chopin wrote so ideally for the piano of the early nineteenth century that the instrument itself seemed ideal and was allowed to remain where it had arrived. He immensely enriched its technique, but compelled no changes in its mechanism. Among the moderns, Ravel and Stravinsky, who write for each instrument as if they played it brilliantly themselves, will enormously advance interpretative skill while leaving manufacture entirely uninfluenced.

Paradoxical though it may seem, it is demonstrably true that the men who cared only for their music and were indifferent to the true claims of the instruments it was written for, were those who called for technical improvements. Bach, whose disregard for his media is evident from the frequent arrangements he made of his music for various instruments and combinations of instruments, was responsible for endless and fruitful discussions among his sons and other successors as to the relative value of the clavichord, the harpsichord and the pianoforte, discussions which led to the progress of the latter and to its ultimate survival as the fittest of the three. Beethoven, who was concerned only with making great music of his piano Sonatas and cared little whether they were good piano music, provoked discontent with their work among the manufacturers, who knew that it would be worth while improving their instruments until they became capable of reproducing the composer's thoughts as adequately as possible. It was in Beethoven's time that the piano finally asserted itself by advancing so decisively that the defeat of its weaker predecessors could no longer be questioned.

Since later history affords ample proofs that music which is great independently of instrumental limitations induced the conquest of these limitations, it may safely be inferred that there must have been some daring and unconventional organ playing at the time of the mediæval endeavours to bring the keyboard within easier reach of the organist. No organ works of the period at which the great polyphonic vocal music began to flourish are known to us, but the instrument itself is sufficient indication to the existence of an important development in organ playing. This may have taken the form of elaborate improvisation—an art which is by nature debarred from perpetuating itself—but even if the organ was used merely to double the intricately contrapuntal singing of the period, the players must have possessed considerable skill and stood in need of greater facilities to exercise it.

The transition from the old unwieldy levers to

the handy keyboard was not accomplished at one bound—hence the impossibility of fixing any definite date to the invention of our modern keys. The gradual transformation can only be roughly assigned to the fourteenth century, and it is believed to have taken its departure in Venice or the surrounding region. But it found helping hands elsewhere. By 1350 a monk of Thorn, in Poland, built an organ with a keyboard that had a complete chromatic scale, and in 1361 a German priest, Nicholas Faber, finished the famous organ at Halberstadt which had a keyboard connected with the pipes over a distance by a roller system and was also provided with all the semitones, placed in a separate row above the diatonic keys. Unlike the modern black keys, they were divided from the latter by a gap wide enough to allow the player, while depressing the upper keys with the finger tips, to control the lower row with the wrists.

During the fifteenth century the size of the keys was reduced several times. As the accidentals gradually assumed their modern position and distinguished themselves in colour from the diatonic keys, the hitherto prevalent habit of marking the keyboard with the lettering of the musical scale

32

fell into disuse. It must have become superfluous much earlier, but like all customs it outlived its original use long after it had become a mere empty formula. We have a similar case in the modern clock. It is quite unnecessary to have its face marked with figures in order to tell the time ; any simple division of the dial into twelve equal parts would serve our purpose as well, but it is not until we see the figures replaced by the letters of a clockmaker's name or an advertisement without the slightest detriment to the clock's utility, that we become aware of their total superfluity.

The full chromatic scale on keyed instruments only became universal after the final abolishment of the ecclesiastical modes and their supersession by the modern major and minor scales in their circle of tonalities. For the earlier, modal system B♭ was the only accidental required,* and it was therefore the single representative of the modern black keys in each octave of the keyboard. A

---

* The use of the B♭ in the church modes as one of the natural harmonic series of the fundamental scale, of which the " leading note " of B♮ does not form part, can only be explained in highly technical terms. Those who are curious to understand the matter should consult the article on *Harmonics* in Grove's *Dictionary of Music*. The article on the *Hexachord* in the same work explains the place of B♭ and B♮ respectively in the church modes.

regal in a picture by Memling, dated 1479, at the Hospital of St. John at Bruges has, however, a keyboard of quite modern appearance, save that the diatonic and accidental keys are of the same light colour and the latter placed farther back than they are to-day. On the other hand, as late as 1619, Michael Prætorius, in his *Organographia,**speaks of organs which have diatonic keyboards with the only addition of B♭ as being still in existence, though out of date. The transformation of the scale, like that of the size of the keyboard, was by no means sudden and did not occur simultaneously throughout Europe.

Once the keyboard had assumed, through an evolution quite disproportionate in length to its obviousness, a normal size with the octave adapted to the natural span of the human hand, it always retained practically the same proportions, which are those still found on the modern piano.

* Part II of *Syntagma Musicum*, published at Wittenberg, 1615-19.

III.   FIRST STRINGED
   KEYBOARD INSTRUMENTS

III. FIRST STRINGED
KEYBOARD INSTRUMENTS

LTHOUGH the preceding chapter deals mainly with the development of the keyboard in connection with the organ, the reader will have gathered that it would be wrong to make the keyed wind instrument unhesitatingly responsible for this most ingenious contrivance for the simultaneous release of a number of musical sounds by a single performer.   Once again, as is so often the case in the early history of musical instruments, we have to be content with what common sense impels us to conjecture.   Seeing that the clumsy nature of the earliest keys was the direct result of the construction of the organ and the disposition of its pipes, the obvious conclusion would seem to be that with the first principle of the key system at any rate, this instrument is to be credited.   On the other hand, the reduction in size of the keyboard to manageable proportions involved problems of adjustment between the scattered organ pipes and the closely-gathered keys which must have been immensely difficult to solve ; it is not unreasonable to suppose, therefore, that it needed the example of other keyboard instruments to sting the organ builder into making an effort to overcome all obstacles in order to reduce his keys to the scale of the human hand.

The theory that stringed keyboard instruments must have already existed before the organ keys became thus adjusted in the fifteenth century is not unsupported by historical proof, though we have to be careful how we adduce it. We must not attach much importance for instance, to the fact that a character in the *Decameron* (1353), on being requested to sing, answers that he would gladly do so if he had a *cembalo* at hand. Most probably a dulcimer or psaltery is meant, though it may be any other instrument misnamed by Boccaccio after the fashion of literary people, who are, and always were, notoriously inaccurate in their musical terminology. As early as 1404, however, Eberhardus Cersne* mentions a *clavicordium* and a *clavicymbalon*, and although the latter may belong to the dulcimer type, the former is certainly a keyboard instrument. Again, in 1511, Virdung† says that he cannot tell who first attached keys to the monochord and who, on

* Eberhardus Cersne, *Der Minne Regel*, 1404.
† Sebastian Virdung, *Musica getutscht und aussgezogen*, Basle, 1511.

account of these keys, called the instrument by the name of *clavicordium*, which shows, if it shows nothing else, that early in the sixteenth century the clavichord was already regarded as an invention of some antiquity.

In trying to fix the earliest date that can be

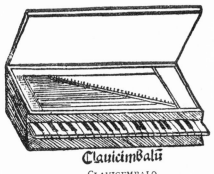

Clauicimßalū

CLAVICEMBALO

assigned to the invention of the clavichord, which we have just learnt from Virdung is a direct off-spring of the monochord, we come upon a description of the latter in a treatise entitled *Musica speculativa* by Jean de Muris, published in 1323, where it still appears, not as an instrument for musical performance, but as a contrivance for the measurement of intervals. The only advance this author suggests is the use of four strings instead of one, which would reduce the instrument's name to an absurdity. The period is, of course, one still mainly devoted to vocal music : instruments were merely mechanical means of support for the voices or at best vehicles for improvisations of which we have no written records. The function of the monochord was simply to give the pitch to the singers, and since to De Muris is attributed the introduction of florid vocal counterpoint, it is by no means fantastic to trace to him an endeavour to improve his instrument to the extent of making it capable of indicating the pitch to four different voices at once—in other words, to strike a four-part chord.

As long as the monochord possessed but one string, it was easy enough to apply to it the tangent that measured off the required note by hand. But now that four tangents had to be pressed to four strings simultaneously, the inconvenience of employing more than one person to do this, to say nothing of the difficulty of pitching the chord accurately, cried out for some automatic subterfuge. The investigations provoked by this need resulted in the keyboard, but by what devious ways it was arrived at and how many clumsy devices were tried until its highly organised mechanism

FIRST STRINGED KEYBOARD

was perfected, no one can tell. By 1450 a clavichord, at any rate in a primitive form, had certainly come into use, but the oldest extant specimen, in the Metropolitan Museum, New York, is dated as late as 1537.

For the method of its tone production the clavichord is unique among stringed keyboard instruments. The tangent, a metal blade fixed upright into the key lever in the interior of the instrument, not only sounds the note, but marks off the length of the string it strikes according to the required note. It follows that the string, when untouched by the tangent, would produce a different, lower note, just as is the case with the violin string that has not been stopped by the player's finger. The close alliance of the clavichord with the primitive monochord is easily perceived. It will now be asked how it is that the tangent, when making the string sound in touching it, does not produce two notes, since it must necessarily set the two lengths of string on either side of it into vibration. This is prevented by the simple expedient of a strip of cloth or felt threaded through the strings behind the point where the tangent comes into contact with them, and by this means the further advantage is gained that the vibration of the whole string is checked directly the key is released and the tangent drops away.

It must be evident that, while the impact of the tangent causes the string to speak, it also damps it to a great extent by remaining pressed against it so long as the note sounds. The exceedingly slender tone of the clavichord is indeed at once its great charm and its great defect. A piece played on this instrument is not so much music as the ghost of music. Compared with it, the harpsichord sounds saucily aggressive, the piano positively brutal, and to the modern ear, focussed to a wider range and an immeasurably greater volume of sound than our ancestors were doubtless accustomed to, it can only appeal under conditions of performance as far as possible removed from those of our modern concert halls. It compensates for what it lacks in body of tone by a tenderness and an intimacy of which no other keyboard instrument is capable. In the case of neither the harpsichord nor the piano does the player remain in direct touch with the sound he produces so long as it lasts, as he does when playing on the clavichord. Once the plectrum has twanged the harpsichord string or the

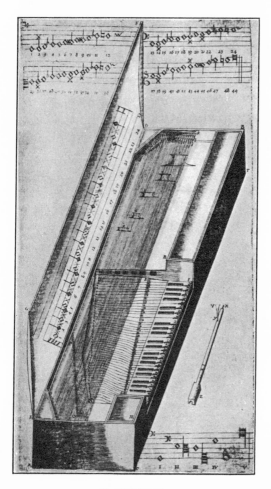

CLAVICHORD.

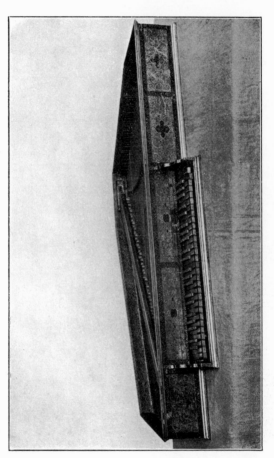

VIRGINAL OF QUEEN ELIZABETH.   *Victoria and Albert Museum.*

hammer struck that of the piano, the performer can add nothing to the quality of the sound, for it has removed itself wholly beyond his control until he strikes the key a second time. Not so with the clavichord, where the finger controls the string as directly as that of a violinist and its sweet and tremulous sound can be distinctly influenced so long as the key is depressed. By shaking the hand gently without withdrawing it, the player can produce an effect not unlike the violin *vibrato*, and the clavichord tone, in spite of its tenuity, has thus a living, breathing character. Power of expression and of dynamic shading, which is almost wholly beyond the scope of the harpsichord and on the piano may only be gained by the shift of giving a succession of notes or chords a certain progressive variety of strength, may in a great measure be exercised over each separate sound on the clavichord. A fugue subject can be made distinctly audible among the subsidiary parts on this as on no other keyboard instrument except the organ. That is why Bach preferred it to either the harpsichord or the piano and why Beethoven, in whose day it was already obsolete, called it the most expressive and controllable of instruments.

ROMANCE OF THE PIANO

A distinction must be made between two kinds of clavichords, the fretted and the fretless variety. The former, which persisted alone until about the first quarter of the eighteenth century, was the only keyboard instrument capable of producing more than one note by means of a single string. As the tangent could be made to strike the string at various points, the early makers saw no reason why two or three adjacent keys with tangents fixed at different distances should not make use of one and the same string. The system had the advantage of reducing the number of strings required and the size of the instrument, but also the much greater drawback that certain notes in close proximity could not be struck together, just as it is impossible on the violin to sound with low G any note less than a perfect fifth above it. It was, of course, not a case of fifths on the fretted clavichord, but only of minor and major seconds, and possibly of minor thirds in extreme cases. One may argue that in any event the old composers had no use for chords containing seconds, but it is more than questionable whether it was not the sheer impossibility of availing themselves of the harmonic effects offered by major and even minor seconds that restrained them from experimenting

FIRST STRINGED KEYBOARD

with them and thus extending their expressive resources. Vocal composers, who had no technical limitations of this sort to reckon with, used clashes of seconds, at any rate by way of suspension, freely, long before the fretless clavichord came into vogue. Nothing is more common in the church music of the time of the fretted clavichord than vocal cadences of this type :—

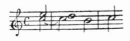

Eventually, a wholesome reform of these restrictions was bound to come. In the meantime, composers were glad if they could have a chromatic scale at their disposal at all, even if all its notes could not be paired together. For the clavichordist was not only during a long period restricted as to chords ; he could not even play a chromatic scale. The earliest instruments of the type had only one black key to the octave, the Bb *, and the possibilities of key variety and modulation were extremely limited. There was, further, a curious curtailment in the bass octave in many of the older instruments. The so-called " short

---

* The reasons for this have already been explained at the close of the preceding chapter, p. 33.

octave " contained only the degrees of the scale
which composers considered necessary to the
bass part of a keyboard piece, where certain notes
were never required. Thus, three adjacent keys
at the bottom of the keyboard might represent,
not contiguous notes of the scale, but, let us say,
C, F, G and B♭, the tonics, dominants and sub-
dominants of C major and F major.* Even in
the later chromatic keyboards B♮ and C♯ were
long omitted in the bass octave, while G♯ was
added last of all.

Arrived at the stage of the chromatic keyboard,
we must leave the clavichord awhile in order to
consider the development of other instruments that
ran parallel with its evolution. This, as will be
seen in a later chapter, had by no means reached
its full fruition at the point at which it could not
only produce a chromatic scale, but chords built
up on any combination of notes selected from it.
The great change that was to revolutionise keyboard music more radically than any other was
the introduction of equal temperament, the
discussion of which must be deferred until all the

* The short octave not only varied a good deal in the instruments of different countries and by different makers, but as
old keyboard instruments have necessarily come down to us
hopelessly out of tune, it is often impossible to do more than
guess the actual tuning of the short octave.

FIRST STRINGED KEYBOARD

earlier facts of our story have been told. For
the moment we must turn back to the time of the
primitive clavichord, or possibly to an even earlier
period, in order to consider the branches of the

Claviciteriũ

CLAVICYTHERIUM OR VERTICAL SPINET

family tree of keyboard instruments which have
not only ceased to bear fruit, as the clavichord
has ceased, but which, owing to the lower
vitality that was theirs from the beginning, have
sunk into all but complete obscurity.

Probably the earliest of all is the clavicytherium,

which is said to have been invented in Italy about
1300. It is here that we first come upon the
distinctive tone production of the harp and the lute
types with the aid of a keyboard. The sound is not
called forth here, as on the monochord and the
clavichord, by a tangent that strikes the string
and remains in contact with it, but by a plectrum
which twangs it for a moment and then leaves it
free to vibrate until checked by a second mechanical device. The monochord, being simply an
implement used for practical purposes by the
masters of church choirs, had no place in people's
homes. It is unlikely, therefore, that the first
keyboard instrument to find widespread domestic
use was its direct descendant, the clavichord.
The people's chief instruments were of the harp
and the lute varieties, especially the latter.
Nevertheless, the church must have exercised
its influence in awakening the need for a domestic
keyboard instrument, for there must have been a
desire in the family circle to reproduce at home
what had been heard and appreciated at divine
service. The gifted music-lover must certainly
have striven to recall the stirring effect of polyphonic choral music in the tranquillity of his own
chamber, and it is obvious that, as this music grew

more and more intricate, the harp and the lute, both of them essentially harmonic instruments, so far used only for improvisation and the imitation of secular songs, were found increasingly inadequate to the reproduction of a combination of contrapuntal parts. The only solution of the difficulty that presented itself was a keyboard, and what is more natural than an endeavour to cut the process of discovery short by adding this new appliance to an already existing type of instrument? The harp and the psaltery, with their numerous strings, lent themselves better to this process than the lute, though even that has a freakish variety with a rudimentary keyboard in the hurdy-gurdy.* The upright position of the harp was at first retained ; the strings were arrayed behind the keyboard at right angles to it, horizontally in the beginning and afterwards vertically.

More mysterious than the clavicytherium is an early instrument which undoubtedly had strings and a keyboard, but whose manner of sound production is not known. It crops up in the literature of several languages : in English it is called

---

* The French *vielle*, not to be confused with the street organ, which is often incorrectly called " hurdy-gurdy."

exchequer, in French *échiquier*, in German *Schach-brett*, and in Spanish *exaquir*, and, as all these names imply, it resembled a chessboard in appearance.* The earliest reference to it occurs in a request for a specimen addressed by King John I of Aragon to his brother-in-law, Philip, Duke of Burgundy; and the same monarch, still casting about for it the following year, sees fit to describe it as a *semblant d'orguens qui sona ab cordes*, from which we may draw the useful inference that keyed string instruments were by no means in general use at that time (*c.* 1390).

Other obscure instruments are the *dulce melos* or *doucemelle*, which appears here and there in Latin countries and may or may not have been the same as the *symphonia* referred to by German writers. Schlick† mentions it and Prætorius‡ devotes to it a whole chapter in which he achieves the remarkable feat of giving the reader no information whatever about it. These minor members of the oldest branch of the keyboard family will

---

* The English etymology seems obscure, but the name of the Court of Exchequer is said to have been derived from a chamber with a chequered floor.

† Arnolt Schlick, *Spiegel der Orgelmacher und Organisten*, 1511.

‡ Michael Prætorius, *Syntagma Musicum*, Wittenberg, 1615-19.

FIRST STRINGED KEYBOARD

never be clearly disentangled : it is impossible
to say whether there were but very few of them,
called by an infinity of different names, or whether
a multitude may have hidden their identity under
one and the same appellation.

IV. THE HARPSICHORD
FAMILY

IV. THE HARPSICHORD
FAMILY

THE harpsichord has several near relations which are often wrongly taken to be independent instruments. The virginal, the spinet and the clavecin, which all belong to the group dominated by the harpsichord, may differ from it in shape or size, much as a grand piano differs from an upright, but fundamentally, as regards their mode of tone production, they are identical with it. One might say that Harpsichord is their common surname, while Virginal, Spinet and Clavecin are the Christian names given to the various members in the different countries where this or that branch of the family was settled. Thus, the virginal's home was England and, according to Prætorius,* the Netherlands ; the spinet is Italian and German, and the clavecin French. Another Italian name for the harpsichord proper is that of clavicembalo† or gravicembalo, which, very inaccurately, points to the connection of the instrument with the dulcimer (now the Hungarian cimbalom), with which it has some-

* Michael Prætorius, *Syntagma Musicum*, Wittenberg, 1615-19.
† Hence the German *Clavicymbel*.

thing in common as regards shape only, but nothing as regards mechanism. And, to make confusion worse confounded, the current Italian abbreviation of *cembalo* brings the name still nearer to the varied nomenclature adopted all over Europe for instruments of the dulcimer type (*cimbalom*, *cymbal*, *cymbalo*, &c.) To curtail the names of these instruments in this manner is as misleading as it would be if a Frenchman used the word *violon* as an abridgment for *violoncelle*. Later, probably after the invasion of England by Italian musicians in the eighteenth century, the name of *arpicordo* also had some currency in Italy.

Needless to say, these different instruments cannot be as exclusively assigned each to its own territory as might appear from the above classification. There was a good deal of exchange between various musical countries. France, for instance, also had the *épinette*, which unfortunately for the bewildered historian was also called *clavicorde* there, as it was called *clavicordio* in Spain. Both these instruments, however, were spinets, that is to say, members of the harpsichord family whose tone is produced by plucking the string, not by striking it with a tangent, as in the clavichord.

HARPSICHORD FAMILY

From the earliest days of their existence the characteristic feature that distinguished the harpsichord types was this method of twanging the strings by means of a plectrum, which came straight from the psaltery, as we have already seen in the case of the clavicytherium. In English the mechanism to which the plectra of keyboard instruments were fixed is commonly called the " jacks."* It was in use from not earlier than the fourteenth century until nearly the end of the eighteenth, when the harpsichord finally surrendered to the piano, and it has of course been resuscitated again in the recent revival of harpsichord making by Dolmetsch, Gaveau, Pleyel and others. The most usual material for the plectrum was a hard quill, but stiff leather was often employed for the jacks controlled by a second keyboard, producing a softer tone to contrast with that called forth by the quills.

In England all quilled instruments from the close of the fifteenth century to about the end of the seventeenth were called virginals. The origin of the name has been variously interpreted. Keyed

* For an early use of the word see Shakespeare's 128th Sonnet. But Shakespeare himself is not free from the demon of inaccuracy that seems to pursue all literary men when they come to deal with musical matters : it is plain that he misuses the word for " keys."

instruments were supposed to be used to accompany the hymn, *Angelus ad Virginem*, and from this it is said to have been derived.* From John Minshen's *Ductor in Linguas* (1617) we learn, on the other hand, that it was so called because virgins and maidens played on the instrument. This author also says that its Latin name was *clavicymbalum* or *cymbalum virginalum*. Thomas Blount, in the *Glossographia*† of 1656, has the following interesting entry : " Virginal (virginalis), maidenly, virginlike, hence the name of that musical instrument called Virginals, because maids and virgins do most commonly play on them." The plural employed here to designate a single instrument is instructive. We often read, in fact, of pairs of virginals‡ where only one instrument is meant. The expression is analogous to that of

* See Chaucer's *Canterbury Tales* (the Miller's Tale) :
> " And al above ther lay a gay sawtrye,
> On which he made a-nightes melodye,
> So swetely, that al the chambur rang ;
> And *Angelus ad Virginem* he sang."

If this interpretation be correct, we have here another example of the loose musical terminology that haunts the literature of all ages : Chaucer speaks of the psaltery.

† " Or, a dictionary interpreting the hard words of whatsoever language, now used in our refined English tongue."

‡ Pepys, Diary, September 2, 1666, describing the Fire of London : " River full of lighters and boats taking in goods, and good goods swimming in the water : and only I observed that hardly one lighter or boat in three that had the goods of a house in, but there was a pair of Virginals in it."

" a pair of scissors " and has been ascribed to the presence of two keyboards in these instruments. This explanation, however, is not very convincing, and sure enough, we have not far to seek for another. Prætorius, writing of the spinet,* which he says is called virginal in England, tells us that it is a small keyboard instrument transposing an octave or a fifth up and placed on the top of a larger instrument. Here we have at once the origin of the custom of speaking of pairs of virginals, which like all customs survived long after it had ceased to be justified, and of the idea of using two keyboards, which means were found later to attach to a single instrument.

Henry VIII played the virginal well and his two daughters Mary and Elizabeth vied with each other in brilliant execution. From the latter's reign, which marked the beginning of the florescence of an unparalleled English school of creative musicians, keyboard instruments were copiously written for by a galaxy of composers, of whom Byrd was the first. But their music existed only in manuscript, though often no doubt a great number of copies passed from hand to hand. The first printed collection of virginal music was not

* Op. cit.

59

published till the year 1611. This was the volume entitled *Parthenia*, containing pieces by William Byrd, John Bull, and Orlando Gibbons.

Excellent virginals were made in England, more especially in the second half of the seventeenth century, when John Loosemore, Adam Leversidge and Thomas White were makers of great fame. Before that time, however, many were imported from abroad, especially from the Netherlands. An amusing letter from Balthazar Gerbier, Master of the Horse to the Duke of Buckingham, written from Brussels in January, 1638, to Sir Francis Windebank, Secretary of State, may be quoted here for the sake of some useful first-hand information it contains :

" Right Honourable,—The Virginall I do pitch upon is an excellent peece, made by Johannes Rickarts att Antwerp. It is a dobbel staert stick as called, hath foure registers, the place to play on att the inde. The Virginal was made for the late Infante, hath a fair picture on the inne side of the Covering, representing the Infantas parke, and on the opening, att the part where played, a picture of Rubens, representing Cupid and Psiche, the partie asks £30 sterling. Those Virginals wch have noe pictures cost £15.—Y^r hon^r will have time enuf to consider on the sum, cause I can keepe the Virginal long enuf att my house. I take my leave and rest, Yo^r hon^{rs}, &c."

To which the "Right Honourable" replies that he does "not much respect the accessories of ornament or paintings," but only that the instru- should be good. Later on, having obtained a virginal, he writes as follows to Gerbier, who obviously knew nothing about keyboard in- struments :

"S^r : The Virginall wch yo^u sent me, is com safe, and I wish it were as usefull as I know yo^u intended it. But the workman, that made it, was much mistaken in it, and it wantes 6 or 7 Keyes, so that it is utterly unserviceable. If either he could alter it, or wolde change it for another that may have more Keyes, it were well : but as it is, our musick is marr'd."

From which we may draw the inference that no standard of manufacture had been arrived at by that time and that construction of each instru- ment and its capabilities depended upon the maker's caprice. The virginal, in fact, was destined never to attain to any fixed pattern, and by the time of Queen Anne's reign it became extinct. The favourite instrument was now the spinet, virtually the same, as we have already seen, but different in form and structure. Whereas the virginal was a small instrument that had to be placed upon the table, a spinet had an oblong form like that of the later so-called square piano and stood as a rule upon its own legs. That is, be it understood, in England at the close of the seventeenth century ; on the Continent the early spinet was often analogous to the English virginal. It reached Germany, Flanders and Brabant from Italy early in the sixteenth century. In 1522 it was established in the household of Margaret of Austria at Antwerp. The etymology of the instrument's name is not clear. It may come from *spina*, which is Italian for thorn, and would thus refer to the quill that plucks the strings, or it may be due to a maker named Spinetti, who worked round about 1500.

In Italy a smaller spinet without legs, tuned an octave higher and called *ottavina* or *spinetta di serenata*, was often placed on a full-sized instrument or could be taken to another part of the room and played, echo-fashion, by a second performer. Here we have a first endeavour to gain variety of tone, which was afterwards achieved by harpsichord makers with the aid of double keyboards and various contrivances resembling organ stops. A wing-shaped spinet was also made with strings running as in the modern grand piano and the keyboard fixed at what is now the curve at the right-hand side of that instrument.

In England there were several famous spinet makers in the seventeenth and eighteenth centuries. In the reigns of Charles I and Charles II Thomas and John Hitchcock, probably father and son, enjoyed a great reputation, while during the Commonwealth they must have had a poor time. There was also Charles Haward, of whom Pepys bought the " espinette " for which he paid £5.*
The English instruments were distinguished from the Continental models by their greater compass, which extended to as much as five octaves. Stephen Keene was the outstanding maker of the transition period from the seventeenth to the eighteenth century, and round about the middle of the latter came Mahoon, Haxby of York and Baker Harris.

Clavecin is simply the French name for the harpsichord, which, the most important keyed instrument preceding the piano, will now have to

* Diary, July 15, 1668

be considered. While the virginal and the spinet were often called, what they in effect were, harpsichords, the latter name was never given to them ; it was exclusively reserved for the harp-shaped instrument which was in fact nothing else at first than a harp manipulated by means of keys, though not uninfluenced in its construction by the pig's-head form of the psaltery.

When the first operas and oratorios were produced in Florence, Rome and Venice round about the year 1600, the harpsichord was already established in the primitive orchestra of the period, for it is a good deal older even than that. The most ancient now in existence is that by a maker who styles himself Hieronymus Bononiensis, dated Rome, 1521, and now at the Victoria and Albert Museum.

The most famous makers of all times are the Ruckers family of Antwerp, who flourished there from about 1579 to 1667. Their name was variously spelt, with the uncertain orthography of the time, Ruckers, Rueckers, Ruyckers, Ruekaers, Rieckers or Rikaert, and was a contraction or corruption of Ruckaerts or Ryckaertszoon or some similar equivalents of the English Richards or

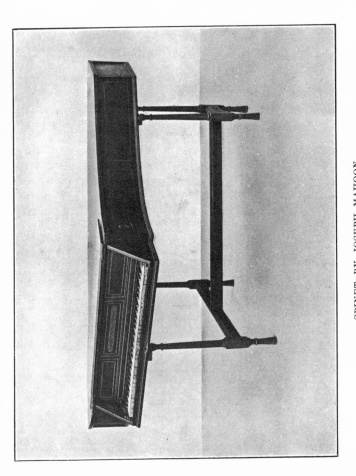

SPINET BY JOSEPH MAHOON.

Victoria and Albert Museum.

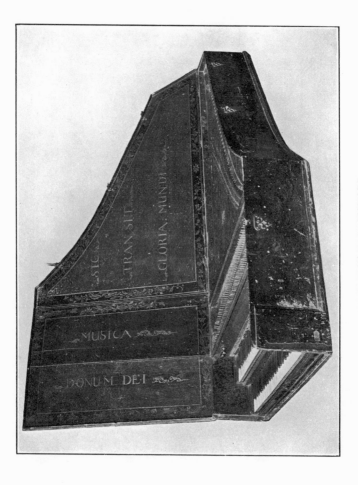

HANDEL'S HARPSICHORD.

Victoria and Albert Museum.

HARPSICHORD FAMILY

Richardson.* After this catalogue of variants of one and the same name we shall have no difficulty in identifying the Johannes Rickarts (one attempt more or less is neither here nor there) mentioned by Gerbier in the letter quoted above as undoubtedly a member of this famous family. They came originally from Mechlin, and the first of them, Hans or Johannes, is credited with having at once made great improvements in the instrument.

The harpsichords bearing the name of Ruckers (to settle down to this most common though probably incorrect version) always enjoyed the reputation of producing the finest tone and their durability was so great that many of them were in use until the harpsichord was finally displaced by the piano, although more than a century had by then elapsed since the last models were made. In England and France Ruckers' instruments a hundred years old were still so well preserved as to make it worth their owners' while to have them decorated with costly paintings. Queen Elizabeth had one of the early models at Nonsuch Palace, and later Handel possessed one by Andries

---

* The Broadwoods, who had some of their instruments for hire, called them Ruker, Rooker or Rouker at different times.

ROMANCE OF THE PIANO

Ruckers, dated 1651.* John Bull, after his appointment as organist at the Cathedral of Antwerp in 1617, a post he retained until his death in 1628, must have been well acquainted with Hans Ruckers and his two sons, Hans and Andries. It is more than likely that the application of double manuals and stops to the harpsichord was the invention of this ingenious family, since they were also organ builders and would thus naturally consider the possibility of making use of these devices to the advantage of stringed keyboard instruments.

Antwerp ceased to be the centre of harpsichord making after the extinction of the Ruckers line, although it had been famous for that industry before their time. As early as 1558 there were no less than ten harpsichord makers in the city. Towards the close of the seventeenth century it lost its reputation to Italy, when Bartolommeo Cristofori† made a great name for himself at Padua. When Prince Ferdinando de' Medici, son of the Grand Duke Cosimo III of Tuscany, a skilled harpsichord player, visited Padua in 1689,

* This is in the Victoria and Albert Museum, and a photograph of it will be seen here. A list of all the extant Ruckers' harpsichords may be found in Grove's Dictionary of Music and Musicians under the article on these makers.
† Sometimes spelt Cristofali.

he induced Cristofori to set up a workshop in Florence. We shall encounter this maker again in an even more important capacity when the time comes to consider the origin of the piano.

Harpsichord making moved to England next. A Flemish maker named Tabel, who had brought the traditions of the Ruckers family to London, employed two foreign workmen who were both to become greater than himself. One of them was Jacob Kirchmann, a German who afterwards adopted the name of Kirkman and who worked under Tabel early in the eighteenth century. A month after his master's death he proposed to his widow and married her within a few hours, establishing himself in Broad Street near Carnaby Market, Soho. He died in 1778 leaving a fortune of nearly £200,000.

His colleague, less adroit in worldly matters, but perhaps more so at his craft, was Burkhardt Tschudi (later half-heartedly anglicised into Burkat Shudi), a Swiss who came of a noble family of Glarus. He was born in 1702 and came to England in 1718 as a journeyman joiner and cabinet maker. Employed by Tabel as foreman, he quickly discovered all the known devices of harpsichord making as well as some hitherto unsuspected. Once he had secured independence for himself, the fame of his instruments quickly spread. He was befriended by Handel and in 1742 styled himself " Harpsichord Maker to H.R.H. the Prince of Wales," his business in Great Pulteney Street, Golden Square, bearing the plume of feathers, while Kirkman's was decorated with the King's arms. Naturally, like their royal patrons, the rival makers were at daggers drawn. Shudi retired in 1772 and died the following year. Samuel Blumer, evidently another Swiss and "late foreman to Mr. Shudi," set up as harpsichord and spinet maker in the same street about 1750 and built upright harpsichords which reverted to the old clavicytherium pattern, though he was perhaps under the impression of having created a novelty. At any rate he effected a saving of space, which of course was the chief aim later of the upright piano.

Both Kirkman and Shudi gave the instrument a more powerful tone than was to be found in the Ruckers and Cristofori models, and they also extended its compass. Each of the two keyboards provided a different sound, generally by the device of fitting one set of jacks with quills and the other

HARPSICHORD FAMILY

with leather plectra. The harpsichord by this time had two pedals, one controlling a contrivance for producing a *crescendo*, in Shudi's case by means of a Venetian blind and in Kirkman's by raising the instrument's lid. The second pedal added or silenced extra strings which automatically enriched the sound by doubling the notes in the octave.

The finest German harpsichord maker was Silbermann, whom we shall also meet again in the chapter dealing with the early pianos. In England the harpsichord made its exit as a concert instrument in 1795, when it was used for the last time at the rehearsal for the King's birthday ode. It was not even allowed to make a dignified last bow on the solemn occasion of the performance, for a grand piano, substituted at the last moment, had edged it ingloriously off the platform.

V. EARLY KEYBOARD MUSIC

V. EARLY KEYBOARD MUSIC

NO useful purpose could be served by an investigation of the history of musical instruments without taking due account from time to time of the development of the art to which they partly gave rise and partly owe their peculiarities. Our narrative has now arrived at a point where it becomes a matter of interest to study the reciprocal relations between the early keyboard instruments and the music written for them, and to try to determine how far manufacture and musical creation affected each other. There are structural features which can only be explained by the demands made by composers for such things as greater range of dynamic expressiveness and variety of tone colour, while on the other side we find technical improvements due to the instrument makers' inventiveness which promptly reacted upon the creative artists by offering them new possibilities of expression. The subject is, of course, a vast one, and only its fringes can be explored in this article, but the reader will perhaps find food for further speculation in the details outlined here.

The give and take between manufacturer and creator may be easily conjectured to have been a constant stimulant to the progress of instrument making and of music as an art from the earliest times, of which we have unfortunately no instruments left, much less written music preserved. The records of composition reach back to less remote time than the early instruments which are still extant, and we have therefore to rely on the latter to give us what evidence they can of the music composed for them—if indeed it was in the strict sense of the term composed, and not merely improvised. From the " short octave " keyboard alone, described in the third chapter, we may gather that the early music must have been greatly limited as to the choice of available tonalities, since there were but very few bass notes obtainable as a foundation whereon a composer could build his harmonic structure. Modulation was restricted to a minimum and chromaticism excluded from keyboard music on the first instruments with their single accidental key to the octave.

It is curious to note that the considerable chromatic licence which composers of vocal music, and especially the madrigalists, allowed themselves with increasing audacity until the madrigal reached an astounding harmonic complexity by the beginning of the seventeenth century, left the early harpsichord music, of which we have printed

records of about the same time, all but uninfluenced. We may judge from this that it was not the
composer so much as the improviser who stimulated makers to the adoption of a complete
chromatic keyboard. A player skilled in the art
of recapturing his impressions at his instrument
would naturally try to reproduce the effect of the
vocal music he had heard and thus come to
demand an instrument on which every semitone
should be available. The curious fact to observe
is that composers actually retained the diatonic
style that was deemed characteristic of keyboard
music, but was in reality only due to the early
defects of the instruments, until long after
chromaticism lay ready to the player's hand.
Thus do conventions perpetuate themselves when
there is no longer any practical justification for
them. For nearly a century after the turning-
point from polyphonic to homophonic music,
which can be conveniently placed at 1600, we
find traces of the old hexachordal system in keyboard music. Even so late a composer as Purcell
uses such an expression as " A Ground in Gamut,"
and Blow has a " Ground in C faut," terms which
at a date so remote from the use of the ecclesiastical
modes in secular music as the late seventeenth

century must have been almost as unintelligible to the lay musician as they are to the amateur of the early twentieth. It is not until the introduction of the tempered scale, which will be dealt with in the next chapter, that we find this antiquated system finally disposed of.

The composition of pieces for stringed keyboard instruments preceded the practice of issuing them in printed form. In England manuscript music circulated particularly freely, as may be judged from the important collections still preserved to-day, such as the Fitzwilliam Virginal Book made for Queen Elizabeth,* sets of MSS. in the possession of noble amateurs like the Earl of Leicester, Lady Nevell† and others, and the book compiled by the composer Benjamin Cosyn‡ from pieces of his own and by some of his most eminent contemporaries. Mary, Queen of Scots, must also have possessed an interesting collection, for she played both the virginal and the lute— " for a Queen, very well," as Sir James Melville tactfully told Elizabeth, who was jealously proud of her own considerable skill in music.

* Published in 1899 by Breitkopf & Härtel.
† Now published by Curwen & Sons, Ltd.
‡ A selection from this book is now published by J. & W. Chester, Ltd.

EARLY KEYBOARD MUSIC

France anticipated England in the matter of publication, for as early as 1560 a *Premier Livre de Tablature d'Espinette* appeared at Lyons. It was, however, not a collection of original keyboard music like the English *Parthenia* of 1611, but merely a set of songs, dances and madrigals adapted to the instrument. The use of dance tunes was peculiar to France in the early days of the keyboard, while the English pieces were at first generally based on songs, elaborated in the form of variations. It is thus to France that we owe the instrumental form of the Suite, which retained the old dance movements until it was displaced by the Sonata and the Symphony— and even there the Minuet persisted. England is responsible for the Variation form, for it was only through French influence that the Suite eventually spread to that country. On the other hand, France owes to England the example of greater elaboration and ingenuity in keyboard composition. When dance tunes were first transferred to keyed instruments in France they were used for their own sake, not as subjects for musical development, whereas English composers at once subjected their material to varied decoration. Nor was the somewhat naïve manner of variation, which was embroidery rather than thematic evolution, the only vehicle used by English composers. Very soon the Fantasia or Fancy came into vogue for the virginal, as it had already been for viols, a freely fugal form often worked out in the most ingenious contrapuntal manner, but not excluding homophonic passages of a florid character. Other pieces, again, had a melody treated in the manner of a *cantus firmus* with independent fugal or ornamental parts playing around it.

From the Variations written for the virginal we may gather some useful hints as to the executive capabilities of the Elizabethan and early Jacobean performers, which must have been considerable, for even to-day, with our advanced technique, we find these works far from easy to perform. The figuration in the variations, taken at the original speed of the tune which it adorns, is often so excessively rapid as to be all but unplayable. We can only conclude that the variations were not all played at the same pace, but since any slackening was obviously made purely from necessity and probably against the composer's intention, it must have been reduced to a possible minimum by conscientious performers and have

TITLE PAGE OF " PARTHENIA " (1611).

JAN STEEN: THE MUSIC MASTER.

National Gallery.

acted as a perpetual inducement to them to perfect
their agility.

In considering the difficulty that confronted the
player of the early keyboard music, we have to
bear in mind the curious and exceedingly clumsy
fingering in use at the time, which must have
involved technical obstacles to smooth execution
of which we can scarcely have any conception.
Mr. J. A. Fuller Maitland, in his edition of
harpsichord pieces by John Blow*—a comparatively late composer—purposely prints one
example with the original directions for the
fingering. The following two passages may be
quoted as characteristic :

(It must be pointed out that the numbering
used here, as it is in the original, is that which, as
Mr. Fuller Maitland with justified indignation
says, " we stupidly call the ' Continental fingering.' " We see that this only rational system of
fingering was as much English as Continental

* J. & W. Chester, Ltd.

79

at that time. What is less admirable however, is that the numeration for the left hand went parallel to that for the right, *i.e.*, the thumb was marked 5).

The thumb, now regarded as the pivot of the pianist's hand, was only used apologetically and never allowed on accidentals.* From Girolamo Diruta (*c.* 1560-1639) we learn more about the queer fingering of the period. He fingers the C major scale as follows for the right hand :

In scale playing Diruta distinguishes between stressed and unaccented notes and makes it an important point that the former should always be played by the fingers marked 2 and 4, the latter by 1, 3 and 5. For some reason or another he calls those marked with even numbers "good fingers" and those with odd figures "bad fingers," the thumb being, to judge from the shabby treatment it receives, by far the worst offender. He goes even so far as to transfer his epithets from the fingers to the notes of the scale, calling the accented notes

---

* One may not speak of "black keys," since the diatonic keys were often black and the accidental keys white.

note buone and the unstressed ones *note cattive*. The neglect of the thumb lasted until the time of Bach, who told his son, Carl Philipp Emanuel, that he had known great players in his youth who never used the thumb except in stretches where it could not be avoided. It was J. S. Bach who raised it from its subordinate position not only to equality with the fingers, but to the rank of their leader, which it still holds to-day, and can never again lose. However, it is evident from Bach's works that he must have retained what was useful in the old technique, which involved not only the curious cross-fingering illustrated above, but also a good deal of gliding from one key to the next with one and the same finger. This expedient is now forbidden by many teachers, but we cannot get very far into Bach's keyboard music without discovering how useful it can still occasionally be in the rendering of old and especially of polyphonic works.

The pianist who performs old music on his own instrument is often worried by the excessive use of ornament on the part of its composers, if he observes their directions too conscientiously. He need not do so, if he bears in mind that the function of grace notes was a purely illusory one and that they were merely the substitute for effects which the harpsichord could not produce, but which are easily within the capabilities of the piano. It must be remembered that the harpsichord tone was entirely uncontrollable by touch. This had the advantage that a scale or other passage played by the most unevenly developed hand still sounded delightfully smooth, but the drawback was that notes could not be accentuated by the player's finger. A subterfuge, a kind of deceptive accent, had therefore to be invented and grace notes, especially mordents, were discovered to serve well in place of accents, while the next best thing to the equally impossible sustaining of a note was found to be the shake. C. P. E. Bach said of the ornaments :—" They bind the notes together ; they animate them ; they give them, whenever necessary, a special expressiveness and weight ; they make them pleasant and therefore attract attention ; they help to explain their intention . . . a mediocre composition may be improved thereby, whilst the best melody must seem empty and clumsy and the clearest substance confused without them."

The knowledge of ornament in old keyboard music is a whole science in itself—one of those innumerable side-tracks which, unsuspected by the layman, lead the student of music into vast fields of special study. Many treatises have been written on the subject by eminent authorities in various countries, among the most important being Diruta's *Il Transilvano*, written in the form of a dialogue between master and pupil (Venice, 1593) ; Couperin's *L'Art de toucher le clavecin* (Paris, 1716) ; C. P. E. Bach's *Versuch über die wahre Art das Clavier zu spielen* (Hamburg, 1753-62); and Marpurg's *Die Kunst das Clavier zu spielen* (Berlin, 1756). The gist of such works is admirably summed up in English by Dannreuther in a voluminous work on the subject.[*] The ornaments current in old English music are to be found clearly tabulated by Wm. Barclay Squire in his complete edition of Purcell's harpsichord works.[†]

Apart from ornament, the player on old instruments had another and even more powerful means of imparting life to his music. This is liveliness of phrasing, without which in fact all music lacks vitality. The modern pianist can, indeed, cheat the hearer to some extent of it by laying stress

---

[*] Edward Dannreuther, *Musical Ornamentation from Diruta to Modern Times*, 2 Vols. (Novello).
[†] J. & W. Chester, Ltd.

on dynamic contrast, but to the harpsichord player it was the very pulse of life. To listen to a fine artist on that instrument, such as Mrs. Gordon Woodhouse, Mme. Wanda Landowska or Mr. Rudolph Dolmetsch, is to realise that they impart life to their music almost solely by the plasticity and refinement of their phrasing.

Pianists who play harpsichord music on their own instrument will do well to keep dynamic expression down as much as their temperament will let them and to pay the utmost attention to phrasing, if they wish to recapture something of the spirit of the old music through a medium so wholly different from that for which it was written. They should cultivate the habit of playing works written for harpsichord or clavichord without the use of the sustaining pedal, for the resulting dryness of the music will compel them to give to every phrase the utmost meaning by modelling it as neatly as possible. On the other hand, if they possess very full-toned pianos, they may find it expedient to keep the damping pedal down throughout the piece : the reduced volume of sound will bring their performance somewhat nearer the illusion of the slender, ghostly voice of their instrument's ancestors. A grand piano may be with little trouble converted into a fairly good imitation harpsichord by covering the strings with a layer or two of newspaper. To play in this way, however, very soon becomes irritating owing to the curiously unpleasant feeling of an unnatural check acting upon one's touch and tone.

Harpsichord music, even in modern editions intended for the pianist, occasionally shows quite clearly how the old instrument's special devices were borne in mind by the composer. There is much evidence of the double keyboards, for instance, in the works of many composers. The frequent repetition of identical phrases played *forte* the first time and *piano* the second, in the Sonatas of Domenico Scarlatti, can only indicate a rapid change from one keyboard to the other. The following passage in Rameau's *La Dauphine* :

was evidently played thus :

ROMANCE OF THE PIANO

The performer, no doubt, was permitted a good deal of licence in making the most of the double keyboards, and must often have produced effects not written down by the composer.* Those who watch Mme. Landowska play Bach's *Capriccio on the Departure of his Brother* will note that she does something of this sort in the *Postilion's Air* :

(The portion here marked " Keyboard I " represents the music as written by the composer ; the left-hand notes on the second keyboard are added by the player.)

Bach possessed a harpsichord that had not only two keyboards, but a set of pedals, on which he could play his organ Trios and other works written for two manuals and pedals. It is clear

* The use of the stops had to be left entirely to the player's discretion, since these mechanical appliances for the production of different tone-colours vary with each maker and almost with each individual instrument.

that his Sonata in D major, among other works,
was written for this instrument. Note this
passage :

which it is impossible to play in its correct note
values with two hands alone. In modern editions
it is generally marked " Pedal," and indeed its
effect can be approximately rendered with the aid
of the sustaining pedal ; but there is no doubt
that this marking took its origin from a confusion
between the piano pedal with the third keyboard,
worked by the player's feet, of Bach's instrument.

To add to these necessarily scanty details the
reader's musical experience will readily supply
other examples showing that the evolution of
music and the development of instruments affect
each other mutually throughout history. The
use of ornaments on the composer's part, for
instance, was not a matter of choice so much as of
necessity dictated by the dynamic inflexibility of
the harpsichord family ; the invention of the

ROMANCE OF THE PIANO

double keyboards, on the other hand, stimulated creative musicians to write more effectively for the instrument, once its resources had been thus enriched ; their enterprise in this direction, again, spurred the performers on to acquiring greater virtuosity ; the players' growing capabilities in turn induced progress both in manufacture and composition ; and so on. Music thus runs in a virtuous circle, its innovations swinging perpetually round from the instrument maker to the composer, from the composer to the performer and from the performer again to the instrument maker.

VI. REVIVAL OF CLAVICHORD
AND BIRTH OF PIANO

VI. REVIVAL OF CLAVICHORD
AND BIRTH OF PIANO

THE narrative of the evolution of stringed keyboard instruments must now be taken up again. The predominant deficiency of the harpsichord that led to the invention of the instrument which was destined to supersede it—unfortunately, for there ought to be room in music for all sorts of instruments of different character—was its inability to achieve gradations of tone except by mechanical means unconnected with the player's touch. The performer's hand could only release a sound of an intensity previously adjusted by the nature of the quill, or at most regulated by stops ; it had, of its own accord, no power to make a distinction between *forte* and *piano* or to produce a transition from one to the other. It was the facility of the new instrument in this direction, which was its most characteristic and valuable feature, that led its makers to give it the name of " Fortepiano," later modified into " Pianoforte."

The clavichord had the advantage over the harpsichord of allowing the player to shade his tone as he went along, but its fundamental weakness of sound precluded it from giving the performer enough scope in that direction as well as from ever gaining a marked ascendancy over the harpsichord. The invention of a new instrument was inevitable. Nevertheless, it fell to the lot of the clavichord to forestall the piano in the achievement of one reform of vast importance without which the advent of the latter instrument would probably have been considerably delayed. This reform was that of the equal temperament, which facilitated the task of the early piano makers very considerably by saving them the hopeless confusion of two conflicting aims which had embarrassed the clavichord manufacturers. The reader will remember that, as has been pointed out in the third article, two types of clavichords were made : the fretted and the fretless variety. The latter, it need hardly be said, was bound eventually to gain complete predominance over the former, owing to the immense advantage that any combination of notes could be struck simultaneously on it, which had been impossible on the fretted clavichord, where one and the same string was often made to serve more than one key.

But now another difficulty presented itself. The new harmonic possibilities naturally urged the more enterprising composers to experiment with them, or at least to transfer to the keyboard instruments such harmonic variety as already lay within their reach in music for voices and for combinations of string instruments. Accidentals began to be more freely used and, as a consequence, the tendency arose to write in, or at least modulate to, tonalities containing many sharps and flats. But here a curious phenomenon interposed itself : the extreme sharp and flat keys sounded distressingly out of tune. This was due to the fact that the more usual keys on the old keyboard instruments were tuned to just intonation.

At this point a short explanation of the term "just intonation" becomes necessary for the uninitiated. If the scale of C major is tuned so on a keyboard instrument as to sound its intervals precisely as they would be played on a string instrument or sung by a vocalist with a very discerning ear, it becomes impossible to tune all the intervening semitones in such a way that, if used as the diatonic notes of a major scale in an extreme key—say B major or Db major—their intervals bear the same relation to each other as those of the C major scale. If, in other words, they are perfectly in tune as chromatic notes in relation to C major, they are not in tune as

ROMANCE OF THE PIANO

diatonic notes among themselves. Or, to put it in yet another way, if B♭ is correctly tuned in just intonation as the fourth note or subdominant of the scale of F major, it will not be possible to use it as A♯ in the scale of B major without distressing the sensitive ear. Again, if the piano were tuned in perfect fifths, as string instruments are tuned, and these perfect fifths were to be continued throughout the circle of keys, thus :—

the octaves would cease to be pure.* A player on a string instrument, which is tuned in perfect fifths, when performing a passage in octave unison simply remedies this deficiency by a slight deviation from the true pitch as taken in relation to the open fifths, but on the keyboard, with its fixed notes, this compromise is not possible.

* For a scientific explanation see Helmholtz, *On the Sensations of Tone as a Physiological Basis for the Theory of Music,* translated by Wm. Ashton Ellis : " When once the Pythagorean division of the octave had been settled, and it had been observed that twelve fifths exceeded seven octaves by the small interval of a Pythagorean comma, the idea of distributing this error among the twelve fifths was obvious. Aristoxenus, a pupil of Aristotle, the son of a musician and writer on music, is said to have advocated this."

Some sort of adjustment, therefore, must be made in the tuning, whether just intonation or what is called equal temperament be chosen as the norm. The old makers, preferring the alternative of just intonation, maintained it for the more usual keys and let the remote tonalities remain out of tune ; but eventually the limitations thus imposed upon music, which in other departments had long advanced beyond them, grew untenable. It became imperatively necessary to adjust the tuning in such a way that the remote tonalities could be used without distressing the ear. This could only be achieved by another subterfuge, which consisted in a slight adjustment of all the chromatic notes in such a manner that the intervals between them bore exactly the same relation to each other—that is to say, the difference in the number of vibrations became equal between all the semitones, which had not been the case in the system of just intonation. The result was, of course, that no interval except the octave was now, strictly speaking, in tune ; but the disparity was so slight as to be almost imperceptible, and the advantage of the intervals of the scales in extreme sharp and flat keys bearing the same relation to each other as the notes in the scale of C major was of immense service in liberating the composer from the old restriction to the few available keys in writing keyboard music.

Needless to say, the new system was not immediately accepted without controversy. String players and singers whose ears were accustomed to just intonation and who perhaps flattered themselves unduly with possessing a keen aural sense at first found equal temperament intolerable, not only because it sounded to them out of tune, but because the regularity of the intervals between every whole tone and semitone in every key struck them as dull and monotonous. A scale of Db major sounded to them too much like a scale of C major in colour and they found it distressing that there should be no difference between, for instance, an F sharp and a G flat.

But the change was inevitable. It is true that many attempts were made, from the earliest times, to place within the range of the keyboard instruments all the notes required by just intonation. As early as 1555 a Venetian, Vito Trasuntino, made a harpsichord based upon an invention by one Nicolo Vicentino, which had only four octaves but no less than thirty-one keys to each, representing not only each diatonic note and each sharp and flat separately, but apparently also double sharps and flats. On this instrument, called *archicembalo*—an arch-harpsichord—key purity was preserved throughout all the tonalities and into the remotest modulations, but it must have been almost invincibly difficult to play. Such experiments, and many of them were made, proved invariably insurmountable obstacles either to the performer or the maker, and not infrequently to both. There was eventually no alternative to the adoption of equal temperament, fiercely as it was contested for a time.

Among those who hailed the appearance of the fretless clavichord with the tempered scale with joy was, first and foremost, J. S. Bach. He argued eloquently in its favour in the most convincing and powerful way a creative musician of his greatness could have done. He wrote, by way of exemplifying the virtues of the new instrument, his great series of Forty-eight Preludes and Fugues, to which, in order to make its application the more persuasive, he gave the title of *Das wohltemperirte Clavier*. The first instrument of the kind has been attributed to Daniel Faber of Crailsheim in Wurttemberg and it is said to have appeared about

97

1720 ; but the first book of the " Well-tempered Clavier " was completed as early as 1722, so that the date, if anything, is placed rather late. Bach showed convincingly that now any of the notes represented by the accidental keys could be used as a starting point for a diatonic scale and music might be written in any of the twenty-four major and minor keys. But that was not all : enharmonic modulation had now become possible. A note that was D$\sharp$ in one chord might become E$\flat$ in the next and the composer be free, as it were, to pass from one key into another by a single step, where previously he would have been obliged to go a long way round by modulating through a number of keys instead of taking the short cut from an extreme sharp key to an extreme flat one, or *vice versa*.

The victory was thus won for modern keyboard music by the tempered clavichord under the inspired generalship of Bach. But although in the way of composition anything could now be done with this instrument, it still had its old defects in the matter of execution. It had indeed greater dynamic expressiveness than the harpsichord, but lacked that instrument's strength and decision of tone. Even its power of expression, however, was

VERMEER   "LADY STANDING AT HARPSICHORD."
National Gallery.

CLAVICHORD BY BARTHOLD FRITZ
BRUNSWICK 1751.

Victoria and Albert Museum.

clearly limited, as we learn from Carl Philipp Emanuel Bach. "While all the other instruments," says that composer, "have learnt to sing, the clavier alone has remained behind in this respect. Instead of fewer and sustained notes, it has been compelled to use a multitude of florid figures, in such wise that one has come to believe that there was good reason to be terrified as soon as one was compelled to play slow or singable music on the clavier."

It became imperative to find a means of combining the strong tone of the harpsichord with the flexibility of the clavichord, but instead of a fusion of the two being attained, a curious thing happened. An instrument came into being, which, although it borrowed its outward appearance and its method of releasing the tone by means of a keyboard from them, differed to all intents and purposes totally from either. What is still more surprising is the fact that it went elsewhere for its most characteristic principle, which is the production of the tone by means of hammers, borrowing it from a much more primitive instrument— the dulcimer. The fame of the virtuoso on that instrument, Pantaleon Hebenstreit, whom we have already met, was responsible for the fact that the first German instruments of the new type actually had their strings set in vibration by hammers striking from above. Nevertheless, the forte-piano owes so much both to the harpsichord and the clavichord that they must be looked upon as standing in the direct line of its ancestry. It is not only its shape and keyboard which it inherited from them; the chief reason why it did not develop directly from the dulcimer, to which it is more nearly allied in the character of its tone production, is the fact that without the example of the clavi-chord and harpsichord, piano makers would have been at a loss to imagine how their hammers could be connected with the keyboard. The in-heritance of the new instrument may be compared to that which is frequently to be observed in human beings, who may derive physical resem-blances from one parent and idiosyncrasies of character from the other.

The actual invention of the piano was long a subject of dispute between Italians and Germans, the latter having in favour of their claims the much larger number of instruments of this type dating from the time of its inception, *i.e.*, the beginning of the eighteenth century. There is, however, no longer any doubt that it is Bartolom-

BIRTH OF THE PIANO

meo Cristofori, the Paduan harpsichord maker settled in Florence after 1689, who is responsible for the discovery of what is now the most widespread of all musical instruments. We have an account of the first four *gravicembali col piano e forte*** made by him in 1709 in an article by the Marchese Scipione Maffei, published in the *Giornale dei Letterati d'Italia* in 1711, containing an illustration of the action which shows that the ingenious Italian had hit at first blush upon a mechanism for the hammers much as it still survives to-day, though of course it took a comparatively primitive and clumsy form. Cristofori was by that time harpsichord maker and custodian of the instruments to Prince Ferdinando de' Medici.

It is true that the term *fortepiano* or *pian e forte* occurs in Italian documents of much earlier date, as far back, in fact, as the records of the family of Este, containing letters from an instrument maker named Paliarino addressed to Alfonso II, Duke of Modena, and bearing various dates of the year 1598 ; but there can be little doubt that this refers merely to a harpsichord with two keyboards,

---

* Three in harpsichord form and one different, probably in the shape of a clavichord or spinet.

controlling hard and soft quills respectively. It was, after all, the obvious designation for any Italian instrument that could be played at will loudly or softly, no matter by what mechanical contrivance, for there is nothing in the name of an instrument called " loud-soft " that has the least bearing upon the nature of its construction.

To Cristofori, then, the honour of having invented the piano will have to remain due until some newly-discovered document definitely invalidates his claim, which is not likely to happen. Germany, on the other hand, may justly pride herself upon her much greater enterprise in taking up the new invention and improving upon it. After Cristofori's death in 1731, few Italians carried on his work. The most important among them was his pupil, Giovanni Ferrini, who in 1730 made a fortepiano for the Queen of Spain (Elizabetta Farnese), who bequeathed it to Farinelli, the singer. Other followers were Geronimo of Florence and Gherardi of Padua.

Among the first Germans to make a fortepiano was Gottfried Silbermann, who about 1736 submitted two of these instruments to Bach. The latter, who to the end of his life always preferred the clavichord, criticised them adversely and

BIRTH OF THE PIANO

Silbermann, much annoyed, desisted for a time from making further experiments. The first Silbermann pianos date from about 1725, and when Bach visited the court of Frederick the Great at Potsdam in 1747, he found several of that maker's instruments in the castle of Sans Souci.* Silbermann was born at the village of Kleinbobritzsch, Saxony, in 1683. He joined his kinsman, Andreas Silbermann—whether a brother or uncle is not known—at Strasburg, but he took no part in the building of the organ for the cathedral there in 1714-16, for he had to leave the city in 1707, having made an attempt to elope

---

* Spitta, in his biography of Bach, confuses the facts remarkably. He says : " Gottfried Silbermann . . . somewhere between 1740 and 1750, constructed two claviers with hammer action, probably after the invention of Cristofori, the Florentine. Bach played on one of these, praised the tone highly, and found fault only with the heavy touch and feebleness of the upper notes. Deeply as Silbermann felt this criticism he nevertheless was willing to bow to it ; he worked for years at the improvement of his hammer action, and at last earned Bach's unqualified praise. It is not likely that Bach ever became the possessor of such an instrument.

" The hammer mechanism did not accommodate itself readily enough to all the appliances of Bach's method of fingering. Still, his satisfaction at Silbermann's instruments shows very clearly whither his clavier music tended."

In placing the date of this occurrence so late as the years between 1740 and 1750, Spitta makes his statement that Silbermann built these instruments " probably after Cristofori " (who died in 1731) look quite absurd. Moreover, Bach died in 1750 and Silbermann himself in 1753, so that the latter could not have worked at his hammer action " for years " after the dates given and then submitted the result to the former.

with a nun. He settled at Freiberg in Saxony, building the cathedral organ there in 1714. He is responsible for no less than forty-seven organs in various Saxon churches. Death overtook him in 1753 while he was engaged in the construction of the Dresden court organ.

Another eminent German maker, who claimed to have been the inventor of the piano and who must at least be given the benefit of the doubt as to whether he can have known the Italian instruments already existing when he devised his hammer action between 1717 and 1721, is Christoph Gottlieb Schröter, born at Hohenstein, Saxony, in 1699. It was he who concluded from Hebenstreit's performances on the dulcimer that hammers alone could ever make an expressive instrument of the harpsichord ; it was he, too, who experimented with the " overstriking " action, *i.e.*, hammers touching the strings from above, and who, emulating the French royal admirer of Hebenstreit, Louis XIV, called his new instrument by the name of *pantaléon*.

A French craftsman, Marius by name, also investigated the use of hammers about the same time as Cristofori, Silbermann and Schröter. In 1716 he submitted the model of an action for

what he called *clavecins à maillets* to the approval
of the " Académie des Sciences " in Paris, but
his object was not to replace the harpsichord so
much as to introduce hammers into it in order to
obviate the troublesome process of requilling.
The Marius action had no damper, so that the
effect of his piano must have been very much like
that of a modern instrument played with the
sustaining pedal permanently depressed. Schröter,
on the other hand, introduced a damper that fell
back upon the string directly the hammer moved
away, instead of remaining raised until the key
was released by the finger. While the Marius
piano failed to check the sound at all until the
vibration of the string naturally came to an end,
Schröter's instrument was incapable of sustaining
any notes. It is difficult to decide which of the
two early types of piano was more unsatisfactory,
but if one considers that the tone must in any
case have been dry and short-lived in those days,
one is inclined to vote in favour of the French
instrument.

VII. CHANGES AND
IMPROVEMENTS

VII. CHANGES AND
IMPROVEMENTS

THE first fortepiano—or piano, as we may now conveniently call it—to be seen in England was, according to Burney, one made in Rome by Father Wood, an English monk. It was the sole representative of the new instrument in Great Britain for several years. The harpsichord makers in England at first adopted a conservative attitude and declared themselves displeased with the new invention ; but before long they had to choose between the alternatives of yielding to the increasing demand for it by adapting themselves to its manufacture, or closing down their workshops. One of the executive musicians who was responsible for the vogue of the piano in England was Johann Christian Bach, who settled down in London in 1759. Johannes Zumpe, a German, who had long worked under Shudi, introduced a new action of his into England in 1765-6. He was also the first to construct small pianos in the shape and size of virginals or spinets : that is to say, to him is due the square, table-shaped piano (often wrongly called spinet) as distinct from the earliest type of piano, which invariably preserved the wing shape of the harpsichord. Zumpe being extremely busy with the manufacture and sale of square pianos and their export to France, another German named Pohlmann established himself in London. It has been claimed that the Zumpe action was really the invention of the Rev. William Mason (1725-97), the poet, composer and writer on church music and the intimate friend and correspondent of Gray. The oldest known Zumpe piano, but not the oldest built by him, is dated 1766. It had black keys divided into two sections, each controlling a different string for the flats and sharps. This is interesting as a proof of the extreme slowness with which the system of equal temperament established its supremacy.

The first public notice of the piano in England is to be found on a Covent Garden playbill of May 16th, 1767, which announces that after Act I of the *Beggar's Opera*, " Miss Brickler will sing a favourite song from *Judith*, accompanied by Mr. Dibdin on a new instrument call'd Piano Forte."

It was only in the second half of the eighteenth century that musicians and makers became definitely aware of a fact which ought to have been obvious to them from the beginning :

namely, that the piano was not a harpsichord or clavichord improved by the substitution of hammers for the quill and the tangent, but altogether a new instrument. The human race is ever hard to reconcile to new conditions ; it clings as long as it possibly can to the belief that they are merely improvements of an old and well-established order of things. Thus the harpsichord maker, rather than regard himself as a piano maker once the new instrument had come into fashion, preferred to continue to be looked upon as a manufacturer of the older type of instrument possessed of enough enterprise or submission to a public craze for novelty to cultivate the piano as a side-line. Even the inventor prided himself rather on having revolutionised the older instruments than on having originated a totally distinct one, while the average composer, as we shall see in a later chapter, continued for some time to write harpsichord music for the piano, quite oblivious of the fact that the latter was so entirely novel a medium as to demand an equally novel style. Even a great genius like Mozart, who as a child had been trained at the harpsichord, did not adapt himself very successfully to a pianistic manner. His keyboard sonatas and concertos are delicious and occasionally sublime music, but they are not essentially congenial to the piano in the sense that his quartets are adapted to strings or his operatic arias to the voice. The truth is, of course, that Mozart came into the world before the harpsichord was extinct and the piano fully developed, and that he could therefore hardly be expected to be either quite off with the old love or wholeheartedly on with the new.

Let us see what kind of a piano it was that Mozart had to deal with. The first instruments of the type known to him were a rather indifferent product by Spaeth, an organ builder of Ratisbon. It was not until 1777, in his twenty-second year, that he wrote the following to his father : " Now I shall have to begin at once concerning the Stein pianofortes. Before I had seen any of Stein's work, I always liked the claviers by Spaeth best ; but now I must give preference to those by Stein, for they damp still better than those from Ratisbon."* Mozart then goes on to say that

* The reader who is familiar with German will be amused by a specimen of Mozart's queer grammar and uncertain spelling, as well as by the old-fashioned style of the letter. The above passage stands as follows in the original :—

" Mon très cher Père !

" Nun muss ich gleich bey die steinischen Piano forte anfangen.

CHANGES, IMPROVEMENTS

Stein is in the habit of exposing his sound-boards to the air, rain, snow, scorching sun, and " the devil and all " (" allen Teufel "), so much so that one should think he would be almost glad if they cracked, and that he afterwards glues the strips of wood together, feeling quite sure that nothing more can happen to them. It is interesting to note that Stein's method is very similar to that adopted by modern makers, especially since the European war, when all the carefully matured wood had to be used for lining the trenches, of seasoning their planks artificially by submitting them to violent changes of temperature until they have done their worst in the way of warping and are incapable of any further mischief.

Apart from the exceptionally good damping contrivance mentioned by Mozart, Stein's pianos had an action improved by the addition of a mechanical escapement, a device whereby the hammer was prevented from falling back the whole distance if one and the same note were struck repeatedly in rapid succession. Although Cristofori had already discovered something of the

Ehe ich noch vom stein seiner arbeit etwas gesehen habe, waren mir die spättischen Clavier die liebsten ; nun muss ich aber den steinischen den vorzug lassen ; denn sie dämpfen noch viell besser, als die Regensburger."

kind, Stein was the first to find means to prevent the successive blows from becoming gradually weaker as they followed quickly upon each other. But that was not all ; he went on progressing. A piano of his dating from about 1780 had the new features of two strings to each note and a lever for keeping the dampers raised by pressure of the knee, which was nothing else but the forerunner of the sustaining pedal.

Johann Andreas Stein was born in the Palatinate in 1728. From 1758 he seems to have been in Paris for some years and he afterwards became organist of the Barfüsserkirche at Augsberg, for which he himself built a new organ. He died there in 1792. The chief imitators of Stein, apart from his heirs, were the Viennese makers Anton Walter and Schanz, the former being one of Mozart's favourite manufacturers, while the latter gained the preference of Haydn. Both also made square pianos in what was then called the English shape, which became fashionable not only in the Austrian capital, but all over the continent of Europe.

The English piano makers, having at last decided to acknowledge that they *were* piano makers and not merely harpsichord builders who found themselves constrained to take an interest in pianos, came into prominence towards the close of the eighteenth century. What Shudi and Kirkman had been to the harpsichord, Broadwood and Stodart now became to the piano. John Broadwood applied himself to the making of a more powerful and sonorous instrument. To his genius are due some of the most important features of the modern piano. As they will be referred to in a later chapter devoted to the piano manufacturers of the eighteenth century which still exist to-day, as the house of Broadwood does, it must suffice to mention here the most important of them. One of these is the method of over-stringing. When Broadwood, about 1775, began to make grand pianos as distinct from the typically English square piano, he lengthened the strings considerably in order to give his instruments greater volume of sound. The consequence was that, to avoid the longer strings producing a deeper tone, their tension had to be greatly increased, to such an extent, in fact, that they would have pulled an instrument constructed in the old and comparatively frail material to pieces. A strengthening of the frame was imperative, but even so the strings, all running in one direction, would have put an undue strain on it, for it was still made of wood at the time. Broadwood then lighted upon the ingenious idea of distributing the tension by using two different bridges, which allowed the strings, divided into two distinct sections, to cross each other. Pulling thus in two directions against each other, they reduced the stress by spreading it over a surface. In 1783 Broadwood patented a less important invention, a double sound-board, with a sound-post between the two planks, as in the violin, which he considered a great advance, but which scarcely had a perceptible effect upon the tone of his pianos.

Robert Stodart opened a piano workshop in Wardour Street in 1776. He is said to have been in the Royal Horse Guards, but, his duties being light, went to learn piano making at Broadwood's, who also occupied him as a tuner. As early as 1777 he patented a hybrid harpsichord-piano, into which he had endeavoured to incorporate the principles of both instruments, which shows that even at this late date they were not yet clearly distinguished in men's minds. This curiosity had a crow-quill register that could be made to take the place of the hammers by

CHANGES, IMPROVEMENTS

means of a pedal. While still at Broadwood's, Stodart had assisted a Dutchman named Americus Backers in the invention of the new action for the grand piano now known as the " English action." It was shortly after the death of Backers that he began piano making on his own account, gaining high repute by his energy and ability. By mutual consent he carried on the manufacture of the grands invented by Broadwood, while the latter reverted to the square piano. Broadwood now set himself to reform the Zumpe model, whose strings were stretched from left to right, as in the clavichord. He transferred the wrest-plank with the tuning-pins to the back of the case, thus letting the strings run from back to front, an innovation which enabled him to straighten out the keys over their whole length, letting them lie parallel with the strings instead of having to twist them about to meet the strings.

A much more radical reform was brought about neither by Broadwood nor by Stodart, but by two obscure workmen employed by the latter : William Allen and James Thom. Greatly plagued by the problem of the still too powerful tension exercised by the strings on the enlarged grand piano invented by Broadwood and taken over by Stodart, they hit upon the bold plan of constructing an iron frame. It seems so simple an expedient that at first sight it may be surprising to learn that it was not resorted to until well into the nineteenth century, for Stodart, who had secured the patent for his firm, only brought it out in 1820. But the problem was not so trifling as it looks, for although it was obvious that an iron frame would withstand almost any string tension, there was no piano made at that time which could itself support the weight of such a frame. It was not until that difficulty was removed by a stronger construction of the outer case of the instrument that the iron interior could be thought of. A still greater difficulty was that the tuning-pins could not be made to hold in an iron frame and the device of boring holes in the iron through which the pins were driven into an inner wooden frame was not a matter to be thought of in a day. Once the principles of Allen and Thom had been found to be practicable, they were soon adopted by every maker throughout the world and they have never again been abandoned.

Although credit for the iron frame is due to these two workmen, an approach to it which at any rate gives a first hint at the idea, was made by

CHANGES, IMPROVEMENTS

James Shudi Broadwood, the son of John. Having extended the keyboard of the piano, he found that the consequently greater extent of the gap between the wrest-plank and the sound-board —the place where the hammers reach the strings from below—had weakened the frame so much that the instrument could not be kept in tune. His remedy was the use of metal bracing or tension bars placed above the strings and bridging over the gap at three different points. This was in 1808 ; ten years later the bars were increased to four.

The evolution of the pedals we owe again to the fertile inventiveness of John Broadwood. Having already devised a method of muting the tone of the strings, if desired, by a kind of organ stop he called " sordin " (anglicised from the Italian *sordino* or the French *sourdine*), which was worked by hand or sometimes by the knee, he transferred it to a pedal. About the same time he thought of controlling the dampers by a second pedal, allowing them to remain raised so long as the foot was kept down, even after the fingers had released the keys. He divided the damper pedal into two sections, which could be depressed together or separately at the discretion of the player, who could thus keep the bass and treble strings undamped independently or together at will. This expedient was retained for about half a century, and its abandonment must be regarded as a distinct curtailment of the instrument's resources.

The muting of the strings by means of a shifting pedal which transfers the hammers so that instead of the three strings they strike only two or one came into general use in Germany before the sustaining pedal was found regularly on every instrument. In Beethoven's early Sonatas the words *con sordini* occur, but he does not indicate any other pedalling.

The development of the action, that most highly organised part of the piano, is of the utmost importance, for it is the direct intermediary between the performer and the source of the sound—the string. The finer its construction, the better will it carry the player's message. We owe its present perfection to several enterprising makers, but none has a greater or more honourable share in it than the Alsatian, Sébastien Erard, who came to England in 1786 to open a workshop for harps and pianos. He took out patents for actions in 1794 and 1801, steadily improving them year by year, until at last, in 1808, he brought out his first repetition action, which enabled the player to strike the same key in rapid succession without risking the interference with the next blow of the hammer's return to position after the preceding one. It was this ingenious mechanism which was at last to lead, in 1821, to his famous and very complicated double escapement action, which remains the basis for the finest grand actions to the present day. By that time Erard had long settled down in Paris.

While England and France were busy ensuring the instrument's progress, Germany was by no means idle. By the end of the eighteenth century the Steins had won the supremacy there which Mozart's appreciation had foretold. Three children of Johann Andreas, the sons Matthäus Andreas and Friedrich, and the daughter Maria Anna, carried on his business at Augsburg after his death in 1792. The daughter, better known as Nanette, was a fine pianist who had played to Mozart when he visited Augsburg in 1777 and she was only eight years of age. In 1793 or the following year she married Johann Andreas Streicher of Stuttgart, an intimate friend of Schiller's, and moved to Vienna, where her husband was appointed professor of music. One of her brothers joining them, they established the Viennese piano manufacture of " Nanette & Andreas Stein " in 1794. In 1802 brother and sister dissolved their partnership and began two separate firms under the name of " Matthäus Andreas Stein " and " Nanette Streicher, geb. Stein." Streicher, although now forty-one years of age—he was born in 1761—changed his profession and, joining his wife in business, took an active share in piano making. This branch of the house eventually became the famous firm of " Streicher & Sohn," the couple's son, Johann Baptist (born 1796), being taken into partnership in 1823. Nanette died in January, 1838, and her husband the following May. Stein of Vienna acquired at least as good a name as his father had done at Augsburg and the house of Streicher became one of the first in Europe. Nanette's immortality is, however, assured chiefly by her friendship with Beethoven. She is the " Frau Streicher " whose name occurs so frequently in that master's letters and who must have possessed an inexhaustible fund of patience. We find Beethoven constantly turning to her in various disagreeable predicaments connected with his

CHANGES, IMPROVEMENTS

endless domestic troubles. She was untiring in producing him medicaments and servants, two commodities of which he constantly complained and as constantly stood in need again as soon as he had got over his disappointment.

VIII. SURVIVING MAKES OF THE 18th CENTURY

VIII. SURVIVING MAKES
OF THE 18th CENTURY

THE history of those who contributed to the invention and perfection of the piano is the history of the instrument itself. So closely are the makers and their work bound up together that it is as impossible to keep the names of the former out of a narrative devoted to the evolution of the latter as it would be to write general history without reference to the human beings through whose efforts and virtues, whose guilt and neglect, whose good or ill fortune, the world's course shaped itself. It may be necessary to revert here in some particulars to facts already outlined elsewhere in this series, but since three chapters are to be especially devoted to a short survey of the careers of the most important establishments who still continue to make pianos, it may be advisable to repeat some information rather than exclude it from the very pages where the reader is most likely to look for it.

For the present, in order to keep at least to a semblance of chronology, only the story of the few firms established in the eighteenth century which still survive and produce keyboard instruments shall be briefly told.

ROMANCE OF THE PIANO

The oldest house of piano makers in the world which still flourishes is that known to-day as John Broadwood & Sons, Ltd. Its career is directly linked to that of Burkat Shudi, the real founder, whose remarkable achievements have already received some attention in these pages. Shudi's first association with the name of Broadwood occurred, quite casually, in 1761, when John Broadwood, a Scottish joiner and cabinet maker who was anxious to perfect himself in the construction of harpsichords, entered his employ. Broadwood was then twenty-nine years of age, for he was born in 1732 at Cockburnspath, a little seaside village in Berwickshire on the border of Haddington. He soon succeeded in winning the entire confidence of his master, who was not slow in realising that he had gained in Broadwood not only a competent assistant, but an original and inventive craftsman, who took a personal interest in the work he did for another and whose suggestions were to be taken seriously. By the time Broadwood had been in Shudi's workshops for eight years, he was found more than worthy to become a member of the family to whom he had been so long and so devotedly attached. John Broadwood married Shudi's daughter Barbara in

L.C. De Carmontelle del.

Delafosse Sculpsit.

LEOPOLD MOZART, Pere de MARIANNE MOZART, Virtuose âgée de onze ans
et de J.G.WOLFGANG MOZART, Compositeur et Maitre de Musique
âgé de sept ans.

THE MOZART FAMILY.

From a Print in the British Museum.

SHUDI TUNING A HARPSICHORD.

By courtesy of John Broadwood and Sons.

1769. The intimate ties thus formed with his employer's household were extended to his trade the following year, when Broadwood became Shudi's partner.

The connection which linked up the two most accomplished harpsichord makers of their time was not to be of long duration, for in 1773 Shudi died. But the house of Shudi & Broadwood, as is was now called, endured. Shudi's son, who was actually christened Burkat and not merely called so, like his father, by a linguistic corruption, succeeded to the latter. It was not until 1782 that Broadwood, now fifty years of age, became sole proprietor of the establishment, which continued to be known as Shudi & Broadwood for a time ; but when in 1795 Broadwood's son, James Shudi Broadwood (born 1772), was admitted to partnership, the style was changed to John Broadwood & Son. Later in 1807, when another son, Thomas, joined the business, the plurality of the junior partners had to be indicated by the addition of an " s " to the name of the house, which has been known ever since as John Broadwood & Sons.

No pianos were made by the establishment until the death of the elder Shudi, whose success with the harpsichord may have induced him to confine himself with a faithful and comprehensible conservatism to the older instrument. But the success of the piano in displacing the harpsichord by its manifold advantages became so insistent that its claim could no longer be ignored without recklessly courting ruin. It was precisely in 1773, the year of Shudi's death, that John Broadwood made his first square piano on the model of Zumpe, which still adhered to the pattern of the clavichord. The eager spirit of invention that animated Broadwood, however, would allow him no rest until he had so far outstripped Zumpe that in 1780 an instrument emerged from his experiments which constituted a new and original model. Among its features were a pedal that raised the dampers from the strings independently of the action and another that introduced a muted effect : they were the forerunners of the two pedals found to-day on every type of piano. These devices were adapted a year later (1781) to the first grand piano built by Broadwood, and he patented them in 1783. To relieve the strain of the strings on the bridge by a principle of counter-action, Broadwood contrived his division of the bridge in 1788. His method of carrying the treble and bass strings on two separate bridges, now known as the overstrung system, was sooner or later adopted by all the other makers.

In 1812 John Broadwood died, not without having seen the dawn of a third generation of descendants in the birth in 1811 of Henry Fowler Broadwood, the child of his son James. Henry succeeded James on his death in 1851, and when he died in his turn, the direction of the firm passed on to a representative of the fourth generation, Mr. Henry John Tschudi Broadwood, the patentee of the " barless " grand piano and one of the first directors of the firm when it was converted into a limited company in 1901.

Until 1904 the Broadwoods remained in Great Pulteney Street, where Shudi had settled a hundred and sixty-two years earlier. It had long been desirable to remove to more spacious and adequate headquarters. The neighbourhood of Golden Square, like the adjacent Soho, once the abode of the fashionable, of doctors and solicitors and well-established citizens of the commercial class, had long become a heterogeneous quarter for small trades, dingy shops and squalid lodgings. It might have gained in picturesqueness what it had lost in dull respectability, but the frequenters of

ROMANCE OF THE PIANO

Regent Street no longer dipped into it, or if they did they needed a very acute historical sense to understand that the presence of a distinguished house in these surroundings was to be traced back to other times. The Broadwoods, whose neigh· bourhood had once held the homes of Mrs. Siddons and Angelica Kauffmann, the birthplace of William Blake, the temporary abodes of Mozart and Madame de Staël, found that their surroundings had slipped by imperceptible stages of deterioration into one of those depressing localities that seem to shrink away from the main streets as if ashamed of their few traces of a past glory even more than of their present sordidness. Traditional pride in a long tenancy had at last to yield to the consciousness that the old premises were no longer fit to harbour a dignified old firm, and a removal became inevitable. In 1904 Broadwoods acquired a spacious building at the corner of Conduit Street and George Street formerly known as Limmer's Hotel, and here, in the more fashionable approaches of Regent Street they opened not only a shop and offices worthy of the oldest piano makers in existence, but also a number of studios occupied by numerous profes- sional musicians. The firm is now in Bond Street.

SURVIVING MAKES

The making of the Broadwood pianos is still continued in accordance with the old principles of the house, whose most valuable tradition is that of never retaining old usage for its own sake, but subjecting it to new developments and improvements whenever they are found justified. The oldest established firm of piano makers might well be excused for resting on its reputation, but the house of Broadwood knows too well that its long career was sustained by very different principles.

The second-oldest of the surviving firms of piano makers is the Paris house of Erard. Its founder, Sébastien Erard, the son of a cabinet maker of Strasburg, was born in 1752. Already in early childhood he evinced a fondness for geometry, mechanics and drawing, gifts which were later to stand him in good stead. That his proclivities were fully matched by enterprise and daring some reckless youthful adventures proved with alarming clearness. At the age of thirteen, for instance, he climbed the bachelor steeple of Strasburg Cathedral and sat on the top of the cross for the sheer pleasure of overcoming a difficulty which others preferred to leave unattempted. By the time he was sixteen, his restless spirit held him at home no longer ; he went to Paris to be apprenticed to a harpsichord maker, who soon discovered that the boy knew more than he could be taught, and found him too inquisitive and independent to be long retained in his service. Erard's next master, on the contrary, appreciated his exceptional gifts so thoroughly that he exploited him in every possible way. The youth having succeeded in turning out a harpsichord of unprecedented excellence, his employer, after first binding him not to claim authorship, brought it out as his own. Erard kept the secret more honourably than this crafty free-booter deserved, but his master, on being plied with questions by clients whose doubts were aroused by this unexpected display of ingenuity, had to confess the truth. Soon Erard's reputation spread throughout Paris, set on foot by the very man who was most anxious to keep it suppressed.

In 1777 Erard found a patroness in the Duchesse de Villeroi, who gave him a workshop at her castle and secured him more leisure than had ever been his before. This privilege he immediately turned to account by working more assiduously than ever and embarking for the first time on experiments in piano making. His earliest attempts were square pianos based on the English models, which were so far the favourite instruments of this type in France.

After three years' work under ideal conditions, this sedulous craftsman determined to open his own workshop, and, in the company of his brother Jean Baptiste, he established himself in the Rue de Bourbon in 1780. Erard's short period of peaceful industry was thus abruptly cut short, for he now plunged into a turbulent sea of competitive jealousy. The instrument makers of Paris, apprehensive of a powerful and already too successful rival, began an elaborate intrigue against him. For some time Erard held his own, but in the end he had to capitulate. As members of the Fan-makers' Guild his enemies enjoyed certain prerogatives which empowered them to seize and close the Erard workshops. Nothing but a royal licence could save the brothers from disaster. Fortunately Sébastien had by this time won the favour of Marie Antoinette, who dabbled in music and was persuaded by a fawning retinue that she sang well. Erard helped to keep up the flattering deception by constructing a transposing piano for the Queen, on which by means of a shifting keyboard any song could be adjusted to the limited compass of her voice. The man who devised so adaptable and obsequious an instrument was worth encouraging, and it was doubtless Marie Antoinette who persuaded Louis XVI in 1785 to come to Sébastien's aid by issuing a warrant permitting him to make " fortepianos " independently of the Guild, although obliging him to employ workmen who satisfied its regulations.

No wonder that under this especial patronage the Erards prospered, so long as royal protection stood for something in a country that was rapidly heading towards the overthrow of its throne. No wonder, either, that they found the favours of the house of Bourbon less desirable by the time it had begun to shake in its foundations. As the Revolution grew more and more inevitable and the royal house tottered more alarmingly day by day, Sébastien, aware that he might with good reason be impeached as a royalist, thought it expedient to pay a visit to Brussels. While he was there, his brother sent word, warning him not to return to Paris. Sébastien thereupon resolved to go to London, the refuge of so many Frenchmen whose loyalty was regarded with suspicion, and with characteristic energy started a branch there. Success did not fail him, and in 1792 he took out a patent for improvements in harps and pianos.

After the Reign of Terror, in 1796, Erard went back to Paris, but he did not close down the London house, with which he kept up continuous communication. The same year saw not only the birth of his nephew, Pierre Erard, who was to become his capable successor, but also the manufacture of the first Erard grand piano. For this type of instrument Erard used at first the English grand action, and it was not until 1809 that he patented his first repetition action for grands— the earliest ancestor of the celebrated Erard action. The Bourbons were no longer, and with them their name had vanished from the thoroughfare where the house of Erard took its departure. The establishment was now settled at No. 13 Rue de Mail, the street where, in the house No. 12, Madame Récamier, the greatest of the "unacknowledged legislators," held her celebrated salon from 1798 onwards.

About this time Sébastien Erard was much occupied with perfecting the harp. There is a story of how, with quixotic magnanimity, he withheld from the market nearly a hundred harps made on a new principle because its success would have spelt certain ruin to a rival maker of the old school. But at last, in 1811, he produced his famous double-action harp, and who knows whether he did not contribute to the evolution of the romantic movement that had by then begun to engulf French art by his dissemination of an instrument that fitted in so well with the prevalent effeminate sentimentality and flaccid idealism? It was said that Erard did not undress for three months before his harp appeared, that he snatched his meals pencil in hand, and that this feverish fit of inventiveness was only broken by an hour's sleep now and again among a litter of papers.

In the meantime Pierre grew up to be an invaluable assistant to his uncle, and in 1821, when only twenty-five years of age, he patented a repetition action of his own in London. It was this ingenious mechanism that eventually became the real model for all modern grand repetition actions, most of which differ from it in some slight particular that endeavours to inflate itself into an original invention, but must all own it as their archetype.

Between 1820 and 1830 the Erards revolutionised the piano. In 1824 Liszt, thirteen years old and a prodigy, played for the first time before a Parisian audience and found the Erard grand a superb instrument, responsive to all his intentions and sensitive to the finest shades of an expressive touch. In France *un Erard* became a synonymous term for a piano, much as nearly a century later " a Zeppelin " came to mean a dirigible airship.

In the Revolution of 1830, which led to the abdication of Charles X, the organ at the Tuileries was destroyed, and Sébastien Erard was appointed to restore it, a task which, needless to say, he did not undertake without seizing every opportunity to perfect the instrument at the same time. But he was struck down by illness before the completion of the new organ, and died on August 5th, 1831, at the Château La Muette, an old hunting box of Louis XV, which the enormous wealth brought in by his inventions had enabled him to acquire for his residence. Pierre Erard, who succeeded his uncle, died in 1855 and left the business to his widow, under whose care it continued to prosper.

Concentration being essential to modern whole-sale manufacture, the London factory was closed down in 1890, and Erard's whole output is now produced by the huge works in Paris ; but the London offices and salesrooms in Great Marlborough Street still constitute an extensive English branch of the house. The Erard has remained the greatest and most perfect French piano, and it is preferred by several artists to any other modern make. It is used exclusively at the Paris Conservatoire, whose first prize, according to an old tradition, is always an Erard grand.

In Germany, the land of great piano makers, curiously enough only one of the important existing firms dates back to the eighteenth century. This is the house of Ibach & Sons. Its founder, Johannes Adolf Ibach, was born at Barmen in 1766. He learnt music and gained a knowledge of the organ and its construction at a monastery, but he eventually became a children's shoemaker. Later on, he turned his attention to the making of pianos, which in those days were not manufactured and exposed for sale at haphazard, but only made to order. With infinite pains and a patience only sustained by his passionate interest in the craft, Ibach made his instruments entirely with his own hands. He was an amateur in the true and literal sense of the term. In 1794, however, he succeeded in establishing a piano and organ manuture in his native town. The undertaking was purely a family venture at first, for Ibach built his instruments with the aid of his wife and daughter. Their annual output would draw a pitying smile from a modern maker, but there was more hard work, tenacity and invincible enthusiasm in early builders such as these than is to be found in a modern factory whose work consists in efficient management and the cold supervision of highly organised machinery. It was a proud boast of the family, contemptible though it may seem now, than in 1811, when the economic situation in Germany was reduced to a pitiable state by the Napoleonic wars, they had turned out and sold no fewer than fourteen pianos.

In 1834 the elder son, Carl Rudolf Ibach, began to take an active share in the family's work, and five years later his younger brother, Richard, followed suit. The concern now began to look something like a firm, and was accordingly given the commercial name of Adolf Ibach und Söhne. At the death of the founder the business was renamed Carl Rudolf und Richard Ibach. In 1869 the younger brother took exclusively to organ building and the piano manufacture became known as Rudolf Ibach Sohn. Carl Rudolf, rightly estimating that he could increase his trade by working from one of the larger centres in the

Rhineland, established a branch at Cologne. As the business flourished and the reputation of the Ibach pianos increased, he was appointed purveyor to the Prussian Court, and in 1880 he was able to open a branch in London.

The last survivor of the eighteenth century is, like the oldest, an English make. The London firm of Collard & Collard grew out of the old-established publishing house of Longman & Broderip. It is true that the name of Collard did not appear until well into the nineteenth century, but the instruments made by the house go back in an unbroken line to the closing years of the seventeen-nineties. Clementi, who was approaching his fiftieth year, having decided to abandon his career as a virtuoso and to go into business as a music publisher, associated himself with Longman & Broderip, and the firm became known as Longman, Clementi & Co. in 1799. It had its main office in Cheapside and branches in the Haymarket and in Tottenham Court Road. To the business of publishing and selling music was added the manufacture and distribution of grand pianos. The firm having gone into liquidation the following year, it soon emerged again as Clementi & Co., and about 1820 it was placed on a more solid foundation by the connection of F. W. Collard with the establishment. Thus, with the aid of a few members of the old firm of Longman & Broderip, the house of Clementi & Collard was launched, and after Clementi's death in 1832 it took the present name of Collard & Collard.

Clementi, experienced musician that he was, became an astute publisher fully acquainted with the tastes of his public. He himself arranged excerpts from the most popular works of the day for the piano, and could also, as a great master of the keyboard, do much to foster the sale of the firm's instruments. He no longer played in public but he still knew how to touch the keys effectively when an instrument had to be shown off to advantage. Perhaps he did not stir the hearts of his hearers profoundly by his virtuosity, but his works, to people who knew as yet little of Beethoven and scarcely dreamt of the coming out-pourings of personal emotion through the medium of the piano, must have seemed replete with feeling. He was one of the transitory composers between the classic objectivity that, broadly speaking, may be said to have ruled the eighteenth century and the introspectiveness of Beethoven and his successors.

IX. THE FIRST REAL
PIANO MUSIC

IX. THE FIRST REAL
PIANO MUSIC

A GREAT deal of what is to-day simply classified as piano music because it is now almost without exception played upon the piano, was never written for that instrument at all. Old composers whose names we find in modern publishers' catalogues under the section headed " piano solo " would fail to understand that term if they could haunt the musical world of the twentieth century. They would be as puzzled by this description as Euripides would be to find his tragedies, in Professor Gilbert Murray's translations, classified under " English literature." If, on asking a music dealer for a copy of Bach's " Well-tempered Clavichord,"* we see nothing ridiculous in his rushing immediately to the shelves where he keeps piano music, it is only because human nature is eternally accommodating to new conditions. Piano music, in the strict sense of the term, cannot well be said to have come into existence before the piano itself became a musical instrument in

---

* It is still generally so called in England, though "Well-tempered Clavier" should be used: Bach did not write expressly for the clavichord or the harpsichord, but simply for keyboard instruments, and his music might be played on either.

general use. It is only by a singular good fortune that music written for keyboard instruments of the harpsichord and clavichord type can now be played on the modern instrument that has superseded them.

To this happy circumstance, however, the fact must be ascribed that neither historically nor æsthetically can a clear dividing-line be drawn between the music for the older instruments and that written for the new one. Composers who worked at a time when the piano had begun to come into vogue without as yet completely displacing the harpsichord and clavichord, could not be expected to find at once a distinctive style particularly congenial to the piano. The Sonatas of Haydn and Mozart must have been played on instruments of the old and the new type, according to whichever happened to be installed in the houses of the music lovers for whom they were intended, although both certainly made tentative efforts at a peculiarly pianistic style, as witness, for instance, Haydn's Fantasia in C major* and Capriccio in G major and Mozart's

* This work gives us a clear indication of the poor sustaining power of the early pianos. Haydn once or twice directs that an octave in the bass be held until the sound has completely died away, an instruction which, if carried out to the letter on a modern piano, would mean well over half-a-minute's wait.

great Sonata in C minor and the Fantasia in the same key that is regarded by some authorities as forming an introduction to it.

It is not, however, until we reach the Sonatas of Beethoven that we find the piano definitely established and catered for specifically : that is, if we choose our examples from the music of the period that still has universal currency, for on pushing our investigations a little further, we find that a very distinctive pianistic style was already well established by the time Beethoven faced the problem, and that the two great pioneers who cleared a path for him were Clementi and Dussek. Both these composers are quite unjustly neglected nowadays, though it is not difficult to account for the circumstance. For one thing, their work is sufficiently like that of Beethoven, whom they both influenced to a considerable degree, to suffer somewhat from the inevitable comparison ; for another, both composers have the misfortune to incur a certain contemptuous dislike of most piano students, the early stages of whose instruction have been made wearisome by the study of their Sonatinas, pieces written frankly for teaching purposes and wholly unrepresentative of their work at its best.

ROMANCE OF THE PIANO

Every pianist who has failed to overcome this unreasonable aversion and whom this chapter may induce for the first time to look up the best of the Sonatas by these two composers may be sure of a pleasurable surprise, for each of them is a consummate master of the pianistic medium.   There is no need even to make allowances for the early stage of development at which the instrument found itself at the time : the Sonatas of Clementi and Dussek belong definitely and for all time to the finest piano music ever written, so long as it is considered expressly as piano music.   From the point of view of the whole art of music they are, needless to say, inferior to those of Beethoven. Neither Clementi nor Dussek has that master's imaginative flight and magnificent gift of formal co-ordination.   As creators they never come near the level of Beethoven's spiritual heights, but their handling of the piano as a musical medium is not equal, but definitely superior, to that master's, who learnt most of what he knew about keyboard effectiveness from these two contemporaries without ever discovering more than a small portion of their secrets.   Beethoven's Sonatas are great in spite of his disregard of the medium ; Clementi's and Dussek's chiefly because they understood it to perfection. Matter being ultimately more important in music than manner, it would be absurd to contest for one moment the overtowering greatness of Beethoven's Sonatas ; all that can be claimed for those of his two minor rivals is that they have the advantage of him in the surbordinate aspect of keyboard handling. But it is to be deplored that two peaks of quite respectable altitude should be unduly diminished in the eyes of man merely because of the overwhelming proximity of a summit of exceptional elevation.

Clementi and Dussek are by no means alike. Each has his distinctive style, his personal defects and his own way even of making the piano yield the utmost in colour and brilliancy of which it was capable in its early days. The Italian's invention is more impassioned and his writing more fiery and full-blooded ; the Bohemian's ideas have more grace and suavity, and his keyboard treatment is distinguished by a limpidness and luminosity that is found in no other music in quite the same quality. Both have humour on occasion, but Clementi's is a sparkling wit that recalls Domenico Scarlatti, while Dussek ingratiates himself by a more heartfelt and less mordant fun. If they have anything slightly in common—

beyond, of course, certain formulas that were the musical small coin of their period—it is a certain shapelessness that disintegrates their sonata movements and makes them curiously unsatisfying considered as musical unities. But even here there is a difference. Clementi can turn shapely themes, but it is in stringing them together that he makes his music run to seed : Dussek has a greater sense of the formal symmetry of a sonata movement, but the subjects from which it is composed too often flounder helplessly towards the end of a metrical period and fail to impress the hearer as clearly-cut sentences. For all their weaknesses, however, the personal distinctiveness and above all the wonderful pianistic manner of these two composers make it incumbent upon every pianist to do his share in repairing the neglect into which they have so unaccountably and undeservedly fallen. Although it is doubtless the more towering genius of Beethoven that effaced these two men of smaller stature, their influence on him must become patent to those who study their work intelligently. In Dussek, moreover, we find a whole range of suggestions that were eagerly adopted by later composers, including Weber, Chopin, Field and many others, and traces of influence extending as far as Schumann, Liszt and even Brahms.*

The first music acknowledged to have been expressly written for the piano was a set of Sonatas by Lodovico Giustini of Pistoia, published at Florence in 1732 and entitled *da cimbalo di piano e forte detto volgarmente di martellatti*.† This is a rare instance for some considerable time to come, of a clear distinction made by a composer between the old and the new keyboard instruments. For the most part the clavier pieces composed between that date and about 1770 were simply harpsichord music which could be equally well played on the new type of instrument, but was not exclusively adapted to its percussive character. One of the few composers who had some feeling for the peculiar nature of the piano was Johann Christian Bach, the youngest son of the great Leipzig cantor, who settled down in London in 1762. The first piano music " that could be properly so called " to be published in England was Clementi's Op. 2, a set of three Sonatas which appeared in 1773. They were written three years

---

* See my study, " The Prophecies of Dussek," *Musical Opinion*, December, 1927, *et seq.*
† " For clavier, loud and soft, commonly called ' with hammers.' "

earlier, when the composer was only eighteen years of age, and the year 1770 may therefore be conveniently fixed as the turning-point in the history of keyboard music at which conscious composition for the new instrument began on a large scale, and the displacement of the clavichord and the harpsichord became an indisputable fact.

Various treatises on keyboard technique written round about the last quarter of the eighteenth century and the first decade of the nineteenth show the gradual realisation on the musicians' part of a transition of style at least as clearly as the music of that period. James Hook's *Guida di Musica*, published some time between 1778 and 1787, is still described as an instruction book for the harpsichord *or* the pianoforte, as if the same kind of tuition would do for either ; the *Klavierschule* of Daniel Gottlob Türk, issued in 1789, shows a dawning awareness of the difference of technique required ; Clementi's *Introduction to the Art of Playing the Pianoforte* (1801) and Cramer's *Instruction for the Pianoforte* (1810) prove that the piano had by that time completely emancipated itself, at any rate in theory, and established a technical legislation of its own. Its code, like all codes adapted to new conditions, was by no means

MUZIO CLEMENTI.

ORCHARDSON: "MUSIC WHEN SOFT VOICES DIE."

without its lapses and errors at the beginning. Even the greatest masters of the keyboard had to learn its peculiarities by degrees.

Technically, that is to say, apart from the question of power and colour of tone automatically provided by the new instrument, the greatest problem that confronted its exponents was that of touch. It did not matter greatly how the keys of the harpsichord were handled, since the weight of touch influenced the strength of the mechanically released tone scarcely more than it does on the organ at the present day. Smoothness in rapid passages was therefore obtainable from that instrument without a corresponding evenness of touch, which now had to be assiduously cultivated in a manner that was bound to change the whole attitude of the musician towards keyboard instruments. Clementi and Cramer were the foremost teachers to see this newly-arisen necessity, but as was to be expected in the case of so unfamiliar a problem, it was not at once satisfactorily solved. It was Clementi who invented the pernicious system of practising with one finger while keeping several keys depressed with the others, a method which, while aiming at finger independence, only locks up the muscles of the forearm and is consequently apt to stiffen the hand. It is he, too, who must be held responsible for the idea of placing a coin on the hand in order to train the pupil to keep it as steady as possible in rapid passages, a device directly contrary to common sense in pianism. If there were brilliant players in those days, this does not so much prove that the system was good as that human ingenuity will occasionally triumph over the most formidable obstacles invented by counter-ingenuity. A performer exceptionally gifted with a naturally good pianistic hand, moreover, would not need to cultivate the bad method extensively enough for it to impair his muscular freedom, and in such cases the teachers of the period probably concluded that, since it was powerless to harm their technique, it must be positively valuable. That many would-be players might have achieved proficiency under different conditions could in the nature of things not be discovered until a new technique was actually tried out very much later.

It is a nice question whether it was a comparatively elementary technique or the undeveloped state of the instrument that accounts for the indisputable fact that even the most accomplished among the earliest pianist-composers

never wrote any music as difficult to perform as
the dizziest pieces of virtuosity by Liszt and
Chopin or, in more recent times, Busoni and
Ravel. Yet we have positive proof that in those
days composers often wrote up to the very limit of
what was then technically possible. The *Non
plus ultra* Sonata by Woelfl openly professes to be
the last word in difficulty, and Dussek's challenge
to it (the *Plus ultra* Sonata, Op. 71, also known as
Le Retour à Paris, Op. 70) claims to go one or
more than one better. Yet both works, though
certainly full of stiff problems for the average performer, are child's play compared with the
Etudes d'exécution transcendante of Liszt or the
Gaspard de la Nuit of Ravel. One can only
conclude that the development of creative and
executive technique proceeded hand in hand with
that of the instrument as a means of performance :
that here, as elsewhere, the histories of composition, of interpretation and of instrumental
evolution are inextricably bound up together.

The famous contest between Clementi and
Mozart in Vienna in 1781 revealed the difference
between the English and the Austrian pianos,
which accounted to a great extent for the diver-
gency between these two composers' respective

styles of playing and even, though in this respect personality counted for a great deal more, in a measure for the dissimilarity between their compositions. The fact that Mozart clung far more rigidly to the old harpsichord style was largely due to the thinner tone of the Viennese pianos and their extremely light touch, which favoured agility at the expense of dynamic colour. The English pianos to which Clementi was used had a much heavier touch that demanded an entirely new technique of blows from the wrist or even the forearm in place of the former scratching or tickling of the keys by a hand scarcely lifted from the keyboard. This percussive manner of playing, combined with the more voluminous tone of which the English pianos were capable, naturally induced a richer, more impulsive and varied style of composition. No wonder that between two such disparate masters of the keyboard the listeners were unable to give a definite preference to either. Of the two rivals who, be it said, profoundly respected each other,* Mozart excelled in immediacy and depth of inspiration when it came to improvising, in tenderness of

* It will be recalled that Mozart, nearly ten years later, used a theme from one of Clementi's Sonatas played during the contest into his Overture to *The Magic Flute*.

158

FIRST REAL PIANO MUSIC

expression and singing touch in melodic passages ;
Clementi in sparkle of passage work, poignancy
of accent and depth of colour.   The English
pianos, it may be remarked in passing, long kept
their supremacy over those made in the Austrian
capital, for when James and Thomas Broadwood
presented Beethoven with one of their grands in
1817, he made no secret of his opinion as to its
superiority.

It will be of interest to give the reader some
specimens of the style of the two most representative figures who exemplify the earliest stages
of piano music that was truly congenial to the
nature of the instrument.   This fascinating
phrase is very characteristic of Clementi's sprightly

invention and pianistic resourcefulness.* The passage is worthy of a Mozart Quartet—note the exquisite free four-part writing—but it is quite impossible to imagine anything so rich and rapidly varying in musical texture, as distinct from musical inspiration, anywhere in Mozart's keyboard work. Another quotation from the Anglo-Italian master may be given for the insight it affords into a specifically pianistic manner that was wholly new in his days.†

Maestoso e cantabile.

That he did not shrink, by the way, from what must have been regarded by his contemporaries as extreme harmonic audacity, may be gathered

* Sonata in G minor, Op. 7.
† Sonata in A major, Op. 26.

FIRST REAL PIANO MUSIC

from the cluster of fifths in the first bar of this example.

In the music of Dussek, who comes slightly later, comparisons with Beethoven rather than with Mozart obtrude themselves, though in point of date— he was born in 1761—he stands a little closer to the latter. Here is a sample which at once shows his astonishingly rich and crowded keyboard writing, his boldness of modulation and a peculiarly Beethovenian habit of delaying the return of an unexpected tonic by prolonging an elaborately harmonised and figured passage over a dominant pedal, which is continued

for some time beyond bars 3 and 4 of this example.*

Another extract may serve to demonstrate with what an almost Lisztian effulgence of changing colour Dussek could at times treat his material.†

The way here chosen of developing a thematic idea by means of presenting it in various forms and keys is also extraordinarily prophetic of Liszt. This last example dates from 1806, when Beethoven had only just arrived at the *Appassionata*, which this work of Dussek's leaves far behind in pianistic luminosity and daring, if in no other respect. It is curious to note here in passing that Dussek's Sonata in C minor

* Sonata in E♭ major, Op. 44.
† Sonata in F♯ minor, Op. 61.

(Op. 35, No. 3) has a most striking resemblance
to Beethoven's *Pathétique*, which was not written
until some five years later.

Hummel also, in a smaller degree, contributed
to the evolution of a creative-executive piano
technique, and among the other pianist-composers
not yet mentioned in the course of this chapter,
who had a greater or less share in it were Steibelt,
Ferdinand Ries, Kalkbrenner, Herz and Thalberg.
The last-named is particularly notable, if not
notorious, for the compliment he paid to Erard's
repetition action by exploiting it in every possible
way and with utter lack of moderation. The
modern pedal technique, foreseen by Beethoven,
was perfected particularly by Chopin and Liszt.
The latter is chiefly responsible for the device of
giving a kind of fictitious enlargement to the span
of the player's two hands by prolonging notes by
means of the sustaining pedal while the fingers
became engaged at some other point of the
keyboard.

X. THE UPRIGHT PIANO—
LAST IMPROVEMENTS

X. THE UPRIGHT PIANO—
LAST IMPROVEMENTS

THE date of the upright piano, which is a comparatively recent invention, may be conveniently fixed at 1800, when Isaac Hawkins of London patented a perpendicular instrument some four feet high and announced it as being of " a more convenient and elegant shape than any heretofore made." The vertical pattern had, of course, been used long before : the clavicytherium, as we have seen, was built in that way.* This belonged to the harpsichord family, but attempts at adapting its form to the piano were made at an early date. In 1739 an Italian maker, Domenico del Mela, made an upright model, Frederici of Gera in Saxony brought out another in 1745, and an Englishman, John Landreth, patented an upright grand in 1787. In 1789 the firm of Broadwood sold a model by another maker " in a cabinet case," and in 1795 William Stodart took out a patent for a piano with a new mechanism which combined the utility of a bookcase with the musical use of this odd piece of furniture, one of the freaks

* See the capital illustration of a 17th century Italian instrument of this type in the third edition of Grove's Dictionary, Vol. I, Plate XIX.

of instrument making whose absurdity was only exceeded by the ridiculous " giraffe " piano that came into vogue soon afterwards.

All these patterns, however, differed in no way from the pianos in table or harp shape, except for the fact that their strings and soundboards were turned up on end, and that a more or less successful adaptation of the old hammer device to the new angle at which the body of the instrument was placed had to be made. The Hawkins upright of 1800 was the first really distinctive instrument made in the new shape and conforming to new conditions.

So far the strings had been merely placed at a right angle from the keyboard upward ; but now they descended below its level and were struck in the middle by the hammers instead of being touched at one end, with the result that the tone immediately became fuller and freer. The Hawkins model for the first time had the wrestplank with its tuning pins placed at the top of the soundboard, whereas before it had remained nearest the keyboard, i.e., in the position it usually occupied in the horizontal grand. Hawkins, having lighted upon the expedient of carrying the strings to a lower level behind the keyboard, was forced to assign the wrest-plank this new position, since otherwise it would have become too difficult of access to the tuner.

The first Hawkins uprights, owing to the difference in the length between the treble and bass strings, had a top sloping from left to right, but this maker's son, John Isaac Hawkins, who was at that time in Philadelphia, made the instrument level by filling in the triangular space with bookshelves. The elder Hawkins gave further distinction to his cabinet pianos, as this type of instrument was then called, by using coiled strings for the bass registers for the first time.

In 1802 Thomas Loud improved upon the Hawkins model, so far as its outward appearance went, by giving a diagonal direction to the strings, which had hitherto been stretched perpendicularly, portability being "the leading intention and feature." By 1804 James Broadwood had begun to take notice of the new departure and its obvious advantage of saving space. He made a sketch for a cabinet piano of his own devising ; this he gave to William Southwell, who turned his attention to the new requirements of the action, which owing to its changed position had to undergo some drastic alterations. Southwell patented a new damper action in 1807.

Some time between the latter year and 1811, Robert Wornum the younger, convinced that the practical value of the new instrument could be still further enhanced by a reduction of its size, created the diminutive model known as the cottage piano. The French cottage piano came into being in 1815, introduced there by Ignace Pleyel, who also made full-sized uprights for the first time that year. We shall hear of Pleyel again in the closing chapter of this study, devoted to a number of foreign piano manufactures still in existence to-day ; but the name of Wornum being now lost to the industry, one or two biographical details of this maker may be conveniently placed here. He was the son of Robert Wornum (originally Wornham), a publisher and violin maker (1742-1815) and was born in 1780. A strong inclination towards mechanics induced him to give up the clerical career for which he was intended and to go into partnership in 1810 with George Wilkinson, who had a piano business in Oxford Street. Two years later a fire caused the dissolution of the firm, and Wornum established a warehouse and a concert room of his own in

THE UPRIGHT PIANO

Store Street. Although he had built a diagonally strung cottage piano, the " Unique ", in 1811 and the vertically strung " Harmonic " two years after, it was not until 1828 that he perfected his cottage model action to his entire satisfaction. Camille Pleyel introduced it into France, where it came so generally into use that it eventually became known in England as the " French action." Wornum's principle is still used for upright piano actions in France and Germany. In 1829 he introduced the " piccolo pianoforte," a low upright, which had a new action with a very easy touch, and recommended itself by its cheapness and durability. He died in 1852.

Another development, or rather a still further reduction in the size of the cottage piano, was the " Bibi " brought out in 1857 by Antoine Bord of Paris, a model now generally known in France as *pianette*. Bord was born at Toulouse in 1814, and learnt his craft at Marseilles and Lyons, settling in Paris when he was only nineteen years of age. He died in 1888.

By the middle of the nineteenth century at the latest, the upright piano had victoriously established a popularity far in excess of that of the grand pattern, though of course for practical rather than

171

artistic reasons. The London Exhibition of 1851 showed 115 upright models against 56 grands ; the old square piano was represented by only nineteen specimens, and its doom may be said to have been sealed by that time. To-day the sale of grand pianos by such a firm as Messrs. Chappell & Co. is only about ten per cent. of the demand for uprights.

. . . . . .

Having now seen the upright piano attain to something like equal perfection side by side with the grand during the first half of the nineteenth century, we still have to examine various improvements from which they both benefited in the course of an evolution of instrument making spread over the whole of that century, an evolution which one may hope has not entirely ceased even to-day, for all the present excellence of the instrument.

The extension of the keyboard became imperative directly the piano had established itself as a distinctive medium for composition and its astonishing new qualities encouraged creative musicians to allow bolder flights to their imagination. Mozart's concert grand by Anton Walter was still restricted to five octaves, a compass with which the early pianist-composers could not be expected to remain satisfied for long. Beethoven's despotic genius especially proved so exacting that instrument makers were compelled to yield to his demands. In the first movement of his Sonata in D major, Op. 10, No. 3, he makes it perfectly plain that he does not suffer the restrictions of the upper registers in his piano gladly. He writes thus :—

but on repeating the passage, varies it as follows :

What he evidently meant at the first statement of the bar marked " a " was this :—

and it was only the fact that his keyboard stopped short at e'''' which compelled him to break the

173

wings of this soaring phrase. Beethoven's Op. 10 was published in 1798. By 1804 James Shudi Broadwood had arrived at f''''. The full seven octaves were reached about 1850 and they are still maintained by many makers, especially in upright pianos, which is doubtless the reason why composers rarely extend their music even now to the full modern compass that reaches to c'''''. Any further extension in either direction would serve no useful purpose. The bass especially reaches to a depth where, at any rate in the sound-quality of the piano, one semitone is barely distinguishable from the next by the normal human ear. It is not in the least disturbing to hear a low A struck with the octave G's in the final chord of the second piano Sonata by Arnold Bax, who boldly wrote down a note the instrument does not possess.

The iron frame principle was fully worked out some time between 1820 and 1850. When pianos began to be strung with a mixture of brass and iron wires it was found that the tuning could not be evenly maintained unless a very strong metal frame controlled the strings and with iron impartiality resisted their unequally divided tension. But an open frame was not enough, even after the tension was distributed over the surface by the system of overstringing. It was Samuel Herve, a workman at Broadwood's, who, in 1821, hit upon the idea of strengthening the frame by filling up some of its space with a rigid metal plate. James Broadwood tried this in various ways between 1822 and 1827 in combination with his tension bars, and in the latter year definitely adopted a metal plate made all of a piece. In 1831 William Allen patented a cast-iron frame combining plate tension bars and wrest-plank in one single casting, the only wooden part being the portion of the wrest-plank holding the lower end of the tuning-pins. He was anticipated, though not with immediate success, in the United States, where in 1825 Alpheus Babcock had invented a cast-iron frame for his square pianos which, though it proved a failure, laid the foundation for later American successes.

The strings increased in thickness as the frame gained in strength, thus acquiring a more and more full-bodied tone. Their growing tension required additional strengthening of the frame, whose greater resistance in turn allowed for still more powerful strings. There was for a time everlasting dispute of supremacy between these two factors.

175

ROMANCE OF THE PIANO

A softer material had to be found for the covering of the hammers, which had been of leather in the early pianos, as the tone of the instruments increased in volume. It was Henry Pape, in Pleyel's workshops in Paris, who first introduced felt made of rabbit's fur, and this was improved upon by Henry Fowler Broadwood, who used a felt made of sheep's wool instead. The latter method, apart from its technical advantages, was also more humane : a rabbit has to be killed to yield his coat, a sheep only shorn.

The pedals we have already seen to have reached a point of development close to that at which they are still left to-day. One or two inventions falling into the period now dealt with never came into universal use. The only really significant one is that of the third pedal whereby any single note or chord can be sustained at will while the pianist goes on to another part of the keyboard and uses one of the two normal pedals independently. It was the discovery of Xavier Boisselot of Marseilles, who brought it out in 1844, and it has been used again of late by Parisian makers, by the Schiedmayers of Stuttgart and by Steinway of New York. A blind French piano maker, M. Montal, exhibited in London in 1862 a *pédale d'expression* which diminished the blow of the hammers instead of shifting them sideways to reach only a single string for each note. This device was adopted by some makers in America and Germany.

The soundboard is now as a rule made of Roumanian pine, and only wood of one and the same grain is selected for any board. At the Leipzig Fair of 1921 the firm of Grotrian-Steinweg exhibited their " homogeneous soundboard " with which they had experimented for some time. In order to ascertain the acoustic properties of the wood, they at first made X-ray tests, which proved of little value. Afterwards they examined the weight of the wood, particularly its specific weight, and the degrees of its elasticity. Little by little they arrived at a system of using only wood of similar acoustic properties throughout a soundboard, and they claim that the " homogeneous soundboard alone vibrates uniformly with each note over its whole surface." Another advantage is said to be that the tone of any piano can be exactly reproduced in another, the quality of sound produced being the result of precise calculations.

ROMANCE OF THE PIANO

A scientific experiment of a similar nature though made with the strings instead of the soundboard, is the so-called " Aliquot system" patented by the house of Blüthner in 1873. It is a device for increasing the tone vibrations by means of additional strings which, although not struck by hammers, enrich the sound by vibrating freely and reinforcing the harmonic upper partials. This principle was suggested by the sympathetic strings that were a feature of some instruments of the viol family, such as the *viola d'amore*, from about the middle of the sixteenth century until they fell into disuse. In the treble, the sympathetic strings of the Blüthner piano are tuned in unison with the ordinary strings, and in the tenor range an octave higher ; while the bass, which is always inclined to overweight the upper notes of the piano in richness of sound, is left without the duplicate strings.

Blüthner's was not the first firm to experiment with sympathetic strings, but the only one to succeed with them. Complications that might well dishearten the most enterprising inventor had to be faced in regard to the separate bridge over which the extra strings had to be stretched, the position of the hammers and dampers which had

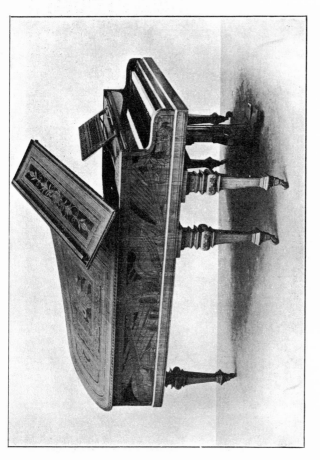

GRAND PIANO BY WORMAN.

DECORATED BY JAMES GAMBLE FOR SIR HENRY COLE, C.B.

Victoria and Albert Museum.

A MODERN PIANO STUDY

to touch the ordinary strings but leave the subordinate ones to vibrate freely, and other problems. But the most formidable task of all was the discovery of a contrivance whereby the sympathetic strings could be tuned automatically with the others, since it is necessary that in order to speak with the latter, the extra strings should be so dead in tune with them that no human ear could arrive infallibly at the correct pitch.

We have to return to the firm of Grotrian-Steinweg for the most recent achievement in piano manufacture, called for by the experiments in composition on a system of quarter-tones by Alois Haba and others. Not feeling justified as yet in attempting the solution of the formidable problem of an actual quarter-tone piano that could render the sub-divisions between the semitones of the ordinary chromatic scale, they made an interesting and successful trial with a keyboard attachment that can be placed in front of the two pianos ranged side-by-side, one being tuned a quarter-tone higher than the other. The attachment, on being played, acts upon the two normal keyboards. An important point is that the new keyboard is of exactly the same dimensions as that to which pianists are accustomed, and that the fingering and the position of the hands remain exactly the same on the black and white keys which still represent the orthodox chromatic scale. The keys for the quarter-tones, of a reddish brown colour, are placed between the black and white keys, which are cut out so as to make room for them, and they slightly protrude in front of the black keys, being thus accessible without the interference of any of the normal keys. Quarter-tone music can now be written for the piano just as it could always have been written for the voice and for string instruments, who indeed, as a certain contralto once proudly declared, have been using them for years.

It would be a fascinating task to describe the process of manufacture of a modern piano, but one that requires not only more space than is available here, but a more specialised technical knowledge than I possess. An interesting illustrated pamphlet on the subject, entitled " The Making of the Steinway," may be obtained from that firm for the asking, I believe, and anyone especially interested would probably not find it difficult to obtain an introduction into one of the great London piano factories. Such a visit is an object-lesson with which no verbal description could compete. It

LAST IMPROVEMENTS

not only gives an insight into the hundreds of details that go to the making of a modern piano, but makes it clear to the spectator why a good musical instrument is so sensitive an organism. It must have often struck anyone who possesses a first-rate piano that it has its days on which it will respond gloriously to the least appeal of the player's touch, others on which it will be coy or remain definitely unresponsive, and yet others on which is positively sulks. The finer its workmanship, the more delicate will be its constitution and the more susceptible will it be to moods : only cheap and worn-out pianos will answer indifferently to everyone who chooses to strum on them ; the best instruments will not yield all they are capable of without some human consideration, for they are almost human themselves.

XI.   SOME FAMOUS
BRITISH MAKES

XI. SOME FAMOUS
BRITISH MAKES

THE story of two English firms of piano makers has already been told in an earlier chapter* devoted to the surviving manufactures established in the eighteenth century. The least invidious and most practical method of relating the careers of the more important houses who sprang into existence during the course of the nineteenth is doubtless that of continuing the narrative in chronological sequence. No order of preference is attempted, for none could do full justice to all the firms whose inclusion in these pages is in itself a tribute to their superiority or an attestation of some particular merit or another. The purpose of this study is not to adjudicate, but to appreciate the dignity of pianoforte manufacture as a whole. Nor is the exclusion of a number of excellent firms to be taken as a tacit depreciation of their work. The plot of this story would only become confused by the adoption of too many characters, and it seemed better to let it unfold itself with the aid of a few leading actors than to cast a large number of players for smaller parts. Some makers have a picturesque history, others a dull

* Broadwood and Collard & Collard, see Chapter VIII.

one, and it is on that account alone that the available space may seem to have been apportioned among them with something less than justice.

The first house to be opened in the nineteenth century was that of Chappell & Co. At the end of 1810, Samuel Chappell, Francis Tatton and John Baptist Cramer came together to frame the plan of setting up a " trade or business of composers of music, music and instrument sellers, etc.," and on January 3rd, 1811, the new firm came into being. Among the three partners, the man who settled down to what he so frankly described as the commerce of composition was doubtless Cramer, one of the most perfect pianists of his time and a conscientious and industrious composer, whose Studies still endure as valuable teaching material. Cramer may have done a good deal of pot-boiling, but he did it at least as well as most creative musicians who regard their work as a mercantile occupation, and there is something engaging in his unabashed announcement of his harmlessly mercenary intentions.

On January 28th, 1811, the *Morning Chronicle* published the following characteristic intimation :

FAMOUS BRITISH MAKES

" Chappell & Co. beg leave to acquaint the nobility and gentry, that they have taken the extensive premises lately occupied by Goulding & Co., 124 New Bond Street, and have laid in a complete assortment of music of the best authors, ancient and modern, as well as a variety of instruments, consisting of Grand and square Piano-fortes, Harps, &c., for sale or hire."

There is a delightful flavour of the time about the frank implication that clients below a certain social standing will not be expected to contribute towards the support of the business. In our more democratic age commercial houses are no longer quite so fastidious as to the sources of their income and even the smartest shops have become remarkably tolerant in this respect.

The select public to whom the new establishment had appealed did not fail to respond, and already in April, 1812, Chappell & Co. were able to extend their business by opening a showroom for instruments specially selected from the best makes by Cramer with the aid of Latour, a well-known professor of music who was interested in the concern. By making of their saleroom an

187

arena where manufacturers could challenge each other with their best products, Chappell's were in a position to assure their noble and genteel clients that the finest available instruments would always be found under their roof.

Samuel Chappell, on his part, had experience in music selling, for he had been with Robert Birchdale at " The Handel House " in Bond Street, one of the few shops in that thoroughfare, which was then partly a residential street.   In 1811 a house could still be offered there with the advantage of being situate in the " preferable part " and with the warning that " persons in business will be objected to."   Lytton's " dear street, of London's charms the centre " was the place for fashionable hotels and libraries, the haunt for beaux to display their shapely legs in tight-fitting breeches, and there was lounging and philandering where now there is hustle on the pavements and perpetual stagnation among the vehicles.   London has no street left that is reminiscent of the pleasant leisure of Bond Street in the days of the Regency : one has to go to Bath, Cheltenham or Tunbridge Wells to find some faint afterglow of this atmosphere of well-bred indolence.

FAMOUS BRITISH MAKES

In January, 1813, Cramer, with Mr. and Mrs. Samuel Chappell as hosts, invited various professional musicians to a gathering, the upshot of which was the foundation of the Philharmonic Society, the first of whose concerts, at which Cramer and his old master Clementi conducted alternately " at the piano-forte," was given as early as March 8th of the same year. At the end of 1813 Cramer withdrew from Chappell's and some time between that year and 1822 the firm removed to No. 50 New Bond Street, where it is still established in premises partly built on the site of William Pitt's garden. The repute of the house now spread to the Continent. In the spring of 1819 Beethoven wrote to Ferdinand Ries : " Potter* says that Chappell in Bond Street is now one of the best publishers." Through Ries he offered them a new piano Sonata and a quintet arrangement. He was just then passing through one of his crises of abject poverty and hoped to make some money by selling a few works to an English publisher and even by visiting England. But nothing came of his plans and, to judge from the date of the transaction, it looks as if the house

* Cipriani Potter, whose studies in Vienna had led to his friendship with Beethoven.

of Chappell had missed the publication of the *Hammerclavier* Sonata in B♭ major, Op. 106.

At the end of 1825 Samuel Chappell and Latour dissolved partnership. The latter remained at No. 50, while the former removed to No. 135 New Bond Street ; but less than five years later, in the course of 1830, Chappell was back at the old address again, having taken over Latour's business. Between 1832 and 1834 two sons, William and Thomas Patey Chappell, entered the business, the latter being taken from school at the age of fourteen to assist his father, who had become blind by this time. Samuel Chappell died in 1834 and left the business to his widow, Mrs. Emily Chappell, who continued to manage it successfully with the aid of her sons. William was an antiquary and historian as well as a publisher. He made collections of *National English Airs* with historical notes, and under his auspices the Musical Antiquarian Society met at 50 New Bond Street for the publication of old English music. Thomas Patey Chappell, whom Gounod called " the Prince of Publishers," was admitted to partnership by his mother in 1856, William having in the meantime left the firm.

Round about the middle of the century the

house began to strike out in a popular line of publication, a policy it still pursues, though music of a different nature is now uppermost in the public favour. Europe was then stricken with the craze for the new dances of the day, which obsessed the public of every capital just as jazz does to-day. The elder Johann Strauss, who visited England in 1849, shortly before his death, held the world spellbound with his waltzes. The polka had just then completed its triumphant sally from its native Bohemia and invaded every European state. So great was its vogue that streets and wearing apparel were named after it and in London public-houses sprang into existence under the name of the " Polka Arms." The fashionable complaint, very likely, was polka legs. Another favourite dance, the music of which could be conveniently abstracted from the current opera repertory, was the quadrille. The composer who wrote and arranged most of the dance music for Chappells' was Charles Louis Napoléon d'Albert, father of the famous pianist.

Before 1850 the house of Chappell had a piano factory in Soho and showrooms in George Street, Hanover Square. The firm brought out as a speciality an instrument combining harmonium

191

and piano, and later, R. A. Kemp, manager of the piano department, invented the Æolian piano, a similar hybrid instrument with but one keyboard and a contrivance whereby the harmonium and piano actions could be made to act separately or in conjunction.

As promoters of concerts Chappell & Co., under whose auspices the Promenade and Symphony Concerts at Queen's Hall flourished until recently, came forward as early as 1858, when St. James's Hall was opened on the site now occupied approximately by the Piccadilly Hotel. The famous " Monday Pops," which lasted until the year 1901, were at first financed and managed by them, with Samuel Arthur Chappell (born 1825) as director. These celebrated chamber concerts, where the finest artists could be heard at the price of a shilling, were perhaps the most vital and ideal activity in the musical life of London for nearly half a century. On the occasion of the thousandth concert Browning wrote a poem for S. A. Chappell, who was familiarly known as " Uncle Arthur."

In 1894 Mr. Edward Chappell, the son of William, engaged Mr. William Boosey to assist him in directing the firm. Mr. Boosey managed the Ballad Concerts at St. James's Hall, as later on he did those at Queen ፥ Hall. He is now managing director of the firm and Mr. T. Stanley Chappell its chairman.

The house of Chappell is in the front rank of British piano manufacturers and one of the most extensive and progressive in the world. The large and well-organised factory attached to it turns out an average of fifty upright and five grand pianos per week. The London house is unrivalled for enterprise and energy, and branches in Melbourne and New York do their share in spreading the reputation of an admirable product of British instrument making.

The firm of Challen & Son, which began to make pianos about 1820, produces an instrument whose superior qualities are combined with moderate prices. This result is attained by a system of standardisation which considerably reduces the cost of production. Instead of turning out some ten or twelve different models, Challens confine their output to four, with the result that greater economy is gained by the wholesale purchase of a comparatively restricted variety of raw materials and a smaller range of

193

machinery is required. This method is perhaps one of the lessons forcibly taught by the European war, during which Challens were allowed to produce only four pianos a week and part of their wood-working machinery was commandeered for aeroplane construction.

A speciality of Challens is an attractive and compact " baby grand " model which in these days of limited dwelling accommodation is particularly welcomed by those who prefer the grand pattern to the upright, but have little room to spare for their instrument. It is often thought that the only advantage of the baby grand over the upright is that the player does not perform with his face turned to the wall, as if he were ashamed of himself. It is argued that, the strings of the diminutive grand being no longer than those of a full-sized upright, the sound cannot be any more powerful. But apart from the fact that the tone of the upright escapes mainly through the back of the instrument and is immediately checked by the wall, it is to be remembered that the upright action, owing to its unfavourable but inevitable position, has never attained to the perfection of the grand action and never yields quite as obediently to the touch. Purchasers who hesitate between the two patterns would do well to bear this point in mind.

We have already seen that in 1813 John Baptist Cramer resigned his partnership in the firm of Chappell & Co. Cramer, who was born at Mannheim in 1771, but was brought to London when only a year old, belonged to that curious fraternity of musicians who reveal equal gifts on the artistic and the commercial sides of their profession. He resembled in this respect Clementi, Diabelli, Kalkbrenner, Pleyel and many other minor composers who have claims to remembrance for two apparently opposed capacities which they knew how to reconcile, and who were not without distinction in either. In the company of Addison & Beale, a small publishing house in Regent Street, Cramer founded a firm of pianoforte manufacturers and music publishers which became known as Cramer & Co., as, after some vicissitudes, it is again known to-day. Securing the music plates of the Harmonic Institution in 1830, these enterprising men increased their catalogue by a large number of important works by great masters and eminent living composers. But they continued to make their own acquisitions of new works and found their " three B's " in Balfe, Barnett and Benedict, whose English Operas they published. In 1844-5 Addison retired and William Chappell joined the firm, which now became Cramer, Beale & Chappell. About the same time they obtained Vincent Wallace's *Maritana*, which was later joined in their catalogue by other works by that faded but once very popular composer. Cramer died in 1858.

As the most influential of piano pedagogues in London, Cramer had no difficulty in finding a large following, not only of pupils but of other professors and through them the piano music published by his firm, including his own celebrated Studies, found a wide circulation. The Cramer pianos were no less successful, and a reputation was thus made which, supported by good workmanship, has lasted to this day.

John Brinsmead, the founder of the famous house of that name, was born in 1814 at Wear Gifford, near Torrington. When he left North Devonshire for London is not on record, but it is certain that he had much experience as a piano maker before he decided to establish himself in the Metropolis in 1836. He made a modest enough beginning in Windmill Street, off Tottenham

FAMOUS BRITISH MAKES

Court Road, but removed to the then stately Charlotte Street near by in 1841. He was soon known to be a tireless explorer and discoverer, who took out patent after patent and added one improvement after another to his instruments. Brinsmead was a passionate lover of his craft and a successful wooer of the charms it held for him. In 1863 a more favourable position had to be sought for the business, and it was found in Wigmore Street. At the same time Brinsmead's two sons, John and Edgar, were taken into partnership and the firm was styled John Brinsmead & Sons. At the Paris Exhibition of 1878 the cross of the Legion of Honour was conferred on the elder Brinsmead. The firm became a limited company in 1900, the brothers John and Edgar Brinsmead being on the board of directors. Once again the legal contraction that stands for "Limited" was affixed to the name of a house which was thus expanding its activities. In the autumn of 1923 the business was transferred to the fine mansion at the corner of Cavendish Square and Wigmore Street, formerly the residence of the Earl of Bessborough. Here, to retain some outward sign of the firm's old standing, a delightful William IV shop front was built on the Wigmore Street side. It is a memorial to the early days of the Brinsmeads, but like all really significant monuments, it symbolises new achievements as much as pride of tradition.

The next firm of importance to be established was that o Rogers & Sons. It was founded in 1843 by George Rogers, an admirable craftsman, whose accomplishments are the more significant because they date back to a time when advertising was not practised as it is to-day. The Rogers piano long ago made its name solely by a degree of quality that ensured it the reputation it still maintains.

After an interval of over forty years, the excellent Spencer piano came into existence in 1884. Already in 1888 it gained the distinctions of a silver medal at the Colonial Exhibition and of two medals at the Melbourne Exhibition. In 1890, though only six years of age, it boldly challenged all British makes, including the most venerable, at the Edinburgh International Exhibition, and won a gold medal. By the time the firm had existed forty years, not far from 80,000 instruments had been sold. The Spencer piano is remarkable for its durability ; even the earliest models still retain their full tone and well-poised touch ; and many of them have successfully come through the severe test of draughts, buffetings, and changes of temperature which pianos are fated to endure on board. For many years, in fact, the Spencer piano has been represented in the British Navy in larger numbers than any other make. Its commercial distribution is under the care of Messrs. Murdoch, Murdoch & Co.

Other fine British pianos are made by the firms of Hopkinson, Marshall & Rose, Allison, Moore & Moore, Eungblut, Strohmenger, etc. It is impossible to continue the list where so much is excellent.

We have seen that during the European war piano manufacture was cut down to a minimum, not only by force of circumstances, but actually by order of the Government. Factories and machinery were freely commandeered wherever they were required, and precious timber, seasoned for many years, had to be sacrificed to the rude purpose of lining trenches. Skilled workmen, needless to say, had to turn their hands to harsher tasks, some of them never to return. Most makers preferred to suspend their activities entirely, but a few of the larger organisations could not do so

199

without facing certain disaster. They reduced their output and expended on it all their ingenuity in finding suitable substitutes for lost or unprocurable material. Pianos of inferior quality resulted, but pianos nevertheless which were astoundingly successful in defying an overwhelming load of adverse circumstances. The firms which did the most heroic work in overcoming all but invincible obstacles, and whose output was thus most numerous and conspicuous, naturally come in for the greatest share of blame, an injustice that is only to be repaired by the acknowledgment that as soon as the variegated and delicate materials required in piano manufacture were again available, a welcome return to the old standards was eagerly made by every maker.

XII.   SOME FAMOUS
                FOREIGN MAKES

XII. SOME FAMOUS
FOREIGN MAKES

A BRIEF historical outline of the pre-eminent foreign piano manufactures established during the nineteenth century* will not take us on an extensive excursion. Paris is to be the starting-point of our itinerary, but afterwards our travels will be mainly confined to Germany, with only a brief visit to Vienna and a voyage or two to America. A great craft, like great art, is a singularly happy coincidence of a series of qualities which a combination of natural endowments with economic circumstances and historical situations happens to produce in certain receptive localities and during certain favourable periods. The wonder is not that great piano makers are confined to four or five countries, but that they are to be found in even as many, for they require the accidental blend of manifold gifts, such as those of the musician, the scientist, the mechanic, the cabinet maker and the business man.

The first make that emerged outside England in the nineteenth century is the Pleyel. Its originator, Ignaz Joseph Pleyel, was born in 1757

* For Erard and Ibach, which belong to the eighteenth century, see Chapter VIII.

as the twenty-fourth child of a village school-master at Ruppersthal in Lower Austria. By what miraculous means his father was able to develop the musical gifts he revealed at an early age is scarcely to be conceived at a time when the upbringing of two or three children strains the resources of men in far better circumstances ; the fact is that the boy was sent to Vienna to perfect himself in piano and violin playing. There he came under the patronage of Count Erdödy, who, in 1774, placed him with Haydn for the study of composition and appointed him conductor of his private band three years later, when he was but twenty years of age. But the young musician wished to see more of the world and obtained leave from his patron to go to Italy, where he continued his studies and became an ardent devotee of Italian opera.

In 1783 Pleyel was called to Strasburg, where he became deputy organist at the Cathedral. After six years' service he succeeded to the post of chapel master. At the end of 1791 he went to London, where he was appointed to direct the " Professional Concerts " during the following season, and there he met his old master, Haydn, again. On his return to the Alsatian capital, he found himself denounced as an enemy to the newly-declared French Republic, and it was to counteract this suspicion, perhaps, that he wrote a Cantata extolling the Revolution. However, he fled the country, and his movements during the next few years are uncertain ; but he eventually succeeded in clearing himself of the charge brought against him and in establishing himself in Paris as a music dealer and publisher some time before 1800.

Pleyel was a fluent and prolific composer, who began well enough for Mozart to praise his Quartets and to express the hope that he would one day replace Haydn. Later on, however, probably because of his activities as publisher, his style became more and more slipshod and imitative, and his early promise remained unfulfilled.

It was in 1807 that Pleyel, who had by this time gallicised his first name into Ignace, opened his piano factory. Unlike Erard, he was neither a cabinet maker nor a mechanic, but he had the good fortune to secure an excellent workman in Henry Pape, who placed his inventive ingenuity and technical skill freely at his master's disposal. Pleyel's son, Camille, who was born at Strasburg in 1788, became partner in the business in 1821 and took it over entirely three years later. The German pianist and composer, Friedrich Wilhelm Michael Kalkbrenner, who was a few years older than Camille and had a reputation as performer and teacher that was likely to benefit the firm, joined it about this time. The elder Pleyel lived in retirement until his death in 1831. The autumn of the same year saw the arrival in Paris of Chopin, who made his début in Pleyel's concert rooms. He liked the easy touch and singing tone of the instruments, which suited his mellow *cantilena* and the gossamer lightness of his elaborate details. The Pleyel piano always retained its character of an ideal instrument for the interpretation of Chopin's music, but it has come down to the present day with the addition of considerable improvements in the direction of power, made by A. Wolff, who later became a partner in the business and occasioned the change of its name to Pleyel, Wolff et Cie. The house has had an agency in London since 1876.

The next piano to originate in the first decade of the nineteenth century came to life at Stuttgart. Its name, Schiedmayer, is now attached to two separate firms, both resident in the capital of

Wurttemberg, but their source is the same. Their remote ancestor is Johann David Schiedmayer, who was a musical instrument maker, first at Erlangen and afterwards at Nuremberg at the end of the eighteenth century and who died in 1806. His son, Johann Lorenz Schiedmayer, born in 1786, went to Vienna in the year of his father's death, and gained experience there as a workman for two or three years. In 1809 he settled at Stuttgart, a place not known to the annals of piano making before that time, and established himself with one C. F. Dieudonné, who died in 1825. The manufacture soon became a great asset to Germany, few of whose important piano makers yet existed at that time. So far Vienna, Paris and even London supplied a great part of its market. Johann Lorenz prospered and in 1845, when his two eldest sons, Adolf and Hermann, were grown up, he took them into partnership. Not long afterwards two younger sons, Julius and Paul, made their studies in instrument making, the latter going to Paris for the purpose. Together they started an independent business at Stuttgart in 1854 and at first confined themselves to the making of harmoniums. After the death of their father in

1860, however, they took to piano making in competition with the older firm. Hermann, the second son of Johann Lorenz, died in 1861 and the earlier house remained in the hands of Adolf and Hermann's son of the same name, under the style of Schiedmayer & Söhne. The younger firm was distinguished by the name of J. & P. Schiedmayer, and is now known as Schiedmayer Pianoforte-Fabrik, vormals J. & P. Schiedmayer. The latter's instruments were first introduced into England by Mr. Archibald Ramsden in 1866.

Though it may have been productive of much bitterness in the Schiedmayer family, the competition of the two firms was certainly beneficial to their instruments. At a time when a first-class home product had German trade practically to itself, its maker might easily have been tempted to take the line of least resistance and to remain satisfied with the distribution of an article just sufficiently good to find a ready sale. As it was, each branch of the house incited the other to greater efforts and the result was that the Schiedmayer pianos, by dint of ceaseless research and improvement, acquired a world-wide reputation which both houses still fully justify to-day.

In America, the earliest firm of piano makers

FAMOUS FOREIGN MAKES

still in existence, and the first to come into prominence, is the house of Chickering & Sons, of Boston and New York. The first pianos in the U.S.A., it should be remembered, were made by Benjamin Crehorne of Milton, near Boston, before the opening of the nineteenth century, but they have died out. They were copied from English models, especially those of Broadwood. Crehorne was followed by other makers, but little progress was made until the establishment of the Chickering firm in 1823. A Scotsman named James Stewart it was who gave the impetus to more enterprising manufacture by inducing Jonas Chickering (born 1798) to join him in opening a factory. But Stewart returned to Europe two years later, leaving his young associate to his own resources. Hard work and sound methods of business made Chickering successful in his venture. In 1837 he introduced the iron frame into his square pianos and his adoption of this principle encouraged other makers to follow suit. Chickering was neither the inventor nor the first American maker of the iron frame. The credit for its introduction—whether independently or in imitation of the English makers is uncertain— belongs to Alpheus Babcock, who had served under Crehorne. The caprices of the American climate played havoc with the strings, and Babcock, as early as 1825, made an iron frame for the square piano to give them an unyielding support. He patented this device which, to tell the truth, was not immediately successful ; but it led to improvements by other makers, notably Chickering, and thus provided the basis for the methods now in use in America. The founder of the firm of Chickering & Sons died in 1853, but the house survives to-day as one of the most honoured and prosperous in America.

Our story takes us back to Germany, where the next important make took root. This, as in the case of the Schiedmayers, was again destined to branch out from one original trunk into two main stems : the house of Steinway and that of Grotrian-Steinweg. The founder was Heinrich Engelhard Steinweg, born at Wolfshagen in the Duchy of Brunswick in 1797. The singular combination of his early predilections for music and for cabinet making marked him out for his future career. He married early in 1825 and settled at Seesen in the Harz Mountains as a cabinet maker, but he soon turned his attention to piano making. In 1839 he exhibited his instru-

A MODERN REPRODUCING PIANO.

DRAWING BY GORDON NICOLL.

By courtesy of Messrs. Steinway.

OCHTERVELT: A MUSICAL PARTY.

National Gallery.

ments at the State Fair of Brunswick and they began to achieve considerable success. The business continued to prosper until 1848, when the February Revolution in Paris stirred up unrest in many parts of Germany and Austria and assemblies in various cities demanded a constitutional Parliament, freedom of the press and reforms in the administration of justice. The revolutionary movement in which Wagner became involved at Dresden about this time did serious harm to German trade and Steinweg's business, owing to these and other circumstances, was brought to grief. Nothing daunted, he decided to try a new venture and sailed for New York, his family following him the next year with the exception of his eldest son, Theodor (born 1825), who preferred to remain at home and save what he could from the wreckage of the paternal business. It is at this point that the firm of Grotrian-Steinweg begins to branch off.

The Steinwegs did not immediately fall on their feet on landing in America, and the father and his three sons were obliged to seek work in various piano factories ; but the varied experience this compulsory service brought them of the conditions obtaining in a country that was as yet strange to them, was to stand them in good stead, for in 1853 they were able to join forces in working on their own account once more. The family now Americanised their name in a curiously incomplete way, the father becoming Henry Engelhard, the sons Charles, Henry and William, and the newly-founded firm Steinway & Sons. In 1855 they adapted the American iron frame to the overstrung scale and named the result the " Steinway system." Having begun exclusively with square pianos, they made their first grand model in 1856 and the first upright in 1862, in which year they attracted attention at the London International Exhibition. The sons, Charles and Henry, died in 1865 and Theodor, having disposed of his establishment at Brunswick, came to join his father and surviving brother in New York. A year later these enterprising men built the Steinway Hall. Henry Steinway the elder died in 1871, and the firm opened branches in London in 1875 and at Hamburg in 1880.

The Steinway factory is one of the largest and most efficient in the world and the superb instrument it produces is unsurpassed by any other make in the new or in the old world.

The men to whom Theodor Steinweg sold his

business on his emigration in 1865 were named Grotrian, Helfferich and Schulz, and they began by styling themselves Th. Steinweg's Nachfolger. Friedrich Grotrian had been in partnership with Steinweg since 1856. Before leaving for the U.S.A., Theodor had already adopted the overstrung iron frame of the New York firm, for pianos of that type were made by him from about 1860 onwards. The Brunswick business maintained the reputation of the old house under the new proprietorship, and many German pianists preferred its instruments to any others. Clara Schumann, for instance, used them exclusively at all her appearances in Germany after 1870. In 1872 a complete rupture between the German and the American house occurred. The former introduced various changes into the action and other parts of the instrument to distinguish it from the New York make. In 1886 Wilhelm Grotrian, the son of Friedrich who died in 1860, became sole proprietor of the concern, and in 1895 his sons, Willi and Kurt, became his partners. Wilhelm Grotrian died in 1917, and in 1919 a third factory and new sawmills were finished at Holzminden. An agency in London, entered as a British company, was opened in 1921. At the

Leipzig Fair of the same year the firm exhibited the " homogeneous sound-board," which is described elsewhere, and more recently still their enterprise produced the quarter-tone keyboard.

The chief Austrian make of to-day is that of Bösendorfer of Vienna. The founder, Ignatz Bösendorfer, who was born in 1795, set up in business in 1828. Thirty years later he retired and left his son Ludwig to continue perfecting the instrument, whose reputation increased year by year. In 1872 the firm had gained so much ground that Ludwig was able to erect an important concert hall, the Bösendorfer Saal, which was opened in state by Hans von Bülow, with whom Bösendorfer was on friendly terms, as he was with most of the famous pianists visiting or resident in Vienna. Leschetitzky used the Bösendorfer piano exclusively for his teaching— in other words, a host of the most celebrated younger keyboard artists were brought up on it.

Bösendorfer's trade, not only in Austria, but in Germany, Russia, Italy, Switzerland, and other neighbouring countries was so satisfactory that, unlike all the other great Continental firms, he never made any effort to export his instruments

to Great Britain. But in 1922 the Wigmore
Piano Galleries took over the agency for the
Bösendorfer piano, the great merits of which soon
asserted themselves, for it is now recognized in
English homes and concert rooms as one of the
makes in the front rank.

The famous house of Bechstein was established
at Berlin in 1853 by Carl Bechstein, who was born
at Gotha in 1826. Not until he had made a
thorough study of instrument making, both
theoretically and by practical work, did he decide
to build pianos of his own. At first, like a true
craftsman whose interest lies more in his work
than in its material proceeds, he made his instruments himself. But success soon compelled him
to engage help and by degrees a firm evolved
which now employs thousands of workmen. In
1856 Hans von Bülow inaugurated the first
Bechstein grand piano by playing on it the Sonata
by Liszt. That master himself was presented
with a magnificent grand which Bechstein sent
him to Weimar in 1860, and he returned the
compliment in the form of a copy of his portrait by
Ary Scheffer. In 1861 Bülow wrote to Klind-
worth in London, asking him to recommend the
Bechstein piano for the forthcoming International

Exhibition, at which the instrument was successfully introduced into Great Britain.

The factory grew apace, enlargements and improvements treading on the heels of ever greater demands. A London branch was opened in 1879 and this was followed in 1901 by the Bechstein Hall,* a concert hall for recitals and chamber music similar to one previously erected in Berlin. Carl Bechstein died in 1900 and was succeeded by his sons. The firm is still under the personal supervision of members of the family, who keep a vigilant eye on its products and watch over the preservation of the good name made by sterling qualities.

The Blüthner piano is the last of the celebrated makes whose career is to be outlined in these pages. The originator, Julius Ferdinand Blüthner, was born in 1824 at Falkenhain, near Merseburg. He opened a piano factory at Leipzig in November, 1853, almost simultaneously with Bechstein in Berlin. Not long afterwards the Blüthner piano was introduced into the Leipzig Conservatoire, to be exclusively used soon afterwards at that illustrious and rigorously conservative institution. The patent for the

* Now Wigmore Hall.

FAMOUS FOREIGN MAKES

" Aliquot system " dealt with in an earlier chapter, the most distinctive feature of the Blüthner piano, was taken out in 1873. A London branch was registered in 1896 as a separate English company and there is also a filial house at Hamburg.

Thanks to the sympathetic strings of the " Aliquot system," the Blüthner has a round and sweet tone by which it may be instantly recognized by any ear that is in the least sensitive to tone-colour. This quality of cool, clear sound has always been the concern of the makers, and power, variety and brilliance of tone are considerations subordinate to it, although, needless to say, they too receive attention.

If it be merely a question of merit, many other makes are entitled to a place in this chapter. A few firms that should at least be mentioned by name are Bord in France, Feurich, Römhildt, Rönisch and Paul Werner in Germany ; and Knabe, Mason & Hamlin, Steck and Weber in the United States.

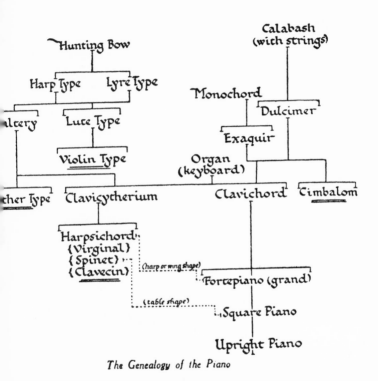

The Genealogy of the Piano

BIBLIOGRAPHY

Bach, Carl Philipp Emanuel. Versuch über die wahre Art das Clavier zu spielen. (New Edition by Walter Niemann.) Leipzig, 1906.

Bie, Oscar. A History of the Pianoforte and Pianoforte Players. (Translated by E. E. Kellett and E. W. Naylor.) London, 1899.

Blüthner, Julius, and Gretschel, Heinrich. Der Pianofortebau. Leipzig, 1909.

Brinsmead, Edgar. The History of the Pianoforte. London, 1889.

Broadwood, James Shudi. Some Notes on the Harpsichord. London, 1862.

Burbure de Wesenbeck, Leo Philips M. de. Recherches sur les facteurs de clavecins et les luthiers d'Anvers depuis le 16e jusqu'au 19e siècle. Brussels, 1863.

Cersne, Eberhardus. Der Minne Regel, 1404. (New Edition by F. X. Wöber and A. W. Ambros.) Vienna, 1861.

Dannreuther, Edward. Musical Ornamentation. London, 1893.

Dolge, Alfred. Pianos and their Makers. Covina, Cal., U.S.A., 1911.

Dolmetsch, Arnold. The Interpretation of the Music of the 17th and 18th Centuries. London, 1915.

Engel, Carl. Catalogue of Musical Instruments (Victoria and Albert Museum). London, 1874.

Fischhof, Joseph. Versuch einer Geschichte des Clavierbaues mit besonderem Hinblicke auf die Londoner grosse Industrie-Ausstellung im Jare 1851. Vienna, 1853.

BIBLIOGRAPHY

Helmholtz, Hermann L. F. von. On the Sensations of Tone as a Physiological Basis for the Theory of Music. (Translated by A. J. Ellis.) London, 1885.

Hipkins, Alfred James. A Description and History of the Pianoforte and of the Older Keyboard Stringed Instruments. London, 1877.

Krehbiel, Henry Edward. The Pianoforte and its Music. New York, 1911.

Marpurg, Friedrich Wilhelm. Kritische Briefe über die Tonkunst. Berlin, 1764.

Mattheson, Johann. Critica Musica. Hamburg, 1722-25.

Mersenne, Marin. Harmonie Universelle, 1636.

Niemann, Walter. Das Klavierbuch. Leipzig, 1918.

Paul, Oscar. Geschichte des Claviers vom Ursprunge bis zu den modernsten dieses Instrumentes. Leipzig, 1868.

Ponsicchi, Cesare. Il pianoforte, sua origine e sviluppo. Florence, 1876.

—— Il primo pianoforte verticale. Florence, 1898.

Prætorius, Michael. Syntagma Musicum. Wittenberg, 1615-19.

Prosnitz, Adolf. Handbuch der Klavier-Literatur, 1450 bis 1830. Leipzig and Vienna, 1908.

Puliti, Leto. Cenni storici della vita del serenissimo Ferdinando dei Medici. Florence, 1874.

Pulver, Jeffrey. Dictionary of Old English Music and Musical Instruments. London, 1923.

Rimbault, Edward Francis. The Pianoforte ; its Origin, Progress and Construction. London, 1860.

BIBLIOGRAPHY

Schlesinger, Kathleen. Articles on Various Musical Instruments in the " Encyclopædia Britannica," London.

Schlick, Arnolt. Spiegel der Orgelmacher und Organisten, 1511. (New Edition. Berlin, 1869.)

Vander Straeten, Edmond. La Musique aux Pays-Bas avant le 19e Siècle, Ghent, 1867-88.

Virdung, Sebastian. Musica getutscht und aussgezogen. Basle, 1511.

Welcker von Gontershausen, Heinrich. Der Flügel, oder die Beschaffenheit des Pianos in allen Formen, Frankfort o / M., 1856.

BIBLIOGRAPHY

INDEX

INDEX

226

INDEX

227

INDEX

INDEX

229

INDEX

INDEX

INDEX

INDEX

INDEX

INDEX

INDEX

INDEX

INDEX

INDEX

239

INDEX

INDEX